GUN CONTROL

AND THE SECOND AMENDMENT

BY CAROL HAND

CONTENT CONSULTANT

ALLEN ROSTRON
PROFESSOR OF LAW
UNIVERSITY OF MISSOURI–KANSAS CITY

Essential Library

An Imprint of Abdo Publishing | abdopublishing.com

abdopublishing.com

Published by Abdo Publishing, a division of ABDO, PO Box 398166, Minneapolis, Minnesota 55439. Copyright © 2017 by Abdo Consulting Group, Inc. International copyrights reserved in all countries. No part of this book may be reproduced in any form without written permission from the publisher. Essential Library™ is a trademark and logo of Abdo Publishing.

Printed in the United States of America, North Mankato, Minnesota
092016
012017

Cover Photo: Don Barens/iStockphoto
Interior Photos: Jessica Hill/AP Images, 4–5; John Minchillo/AP Images, 9; Mike Groll/AP Images, 14–15; Steve Ikeguchi/Shutterstock Images, 20; North Wind Picture Archives, 24–25, 27; Will Vragovic/The Tampa Bay Times/AP Images, 32; Brady's National Photographic Portrait Galleries/Library of Congress, 34–35; Everett Collection, 37; Duricka/AP Images, 40; Ira Bostic/Shutterstock Images, 45; Steve Helber/AP Images, 46–47; Phelan M. Ebenhack/AP Images, 55; Patsy Lynch/Polaris/ Newscom, 56–57; Reed Saxon/AP Images, 61; Tom Williams/CQ Roll Call/AP Images, 66–67; Red Line Editorial, 69, 81; Christian Gooden/St. Louis Post-Dispatch/AP Images, 71; LNP/Rex Features/AP Images, 77; Carlos Osorio/Toronto Star/Getty Images, 78–79; Rick Rycroft/AP Images, 83; Abir Sultan/EPA/Newscom, 87; Susan Walsh/AP Images, 90–91; Jae C. Hong/AP Images, 92; J. Scott Applewhite/AP Images, 95

Editor: Mirella Miller
Series Designer: Maggie Villaume

Publisher's Cataloging-in-Publication Data

Names: Hand, Carol, author.
Title: Gun control and the Second Amendment / by Carol Hand.
Description: Minneapolis, MN : Abdo Publishing, 2017. | Series: Special reports |
    Includes bibliographical references and index.
Identifiers: LCCN 2016945215 | ISBN 9781680783957 (lib. bdg.) |
    ISBN 9781680797480 (ebook)
Subjects: LCSH: Gun control--United States--Juvenile literature. | Firearms
    ownership--Government policy--United States--Juvenile literature.
Classification: DDC 363.330973--dc23
LC record available at http://lccn.loc.gov/2016945215

CONTENTS

CHAPTER ONE

MASSACRE AT
SANDY HOOK

Friday, December 14, 2012, started out as a normal day in Newtown, Connecticut. At Sandy Hook Elementary School, the school's 600 students, kindergartners through fourth graders, had arrived and settled in for the day.[1] They were more excited than usual because of the upcoming Christmas holiday. But at 9:35 a.m., anticipation turned to tragedy. A man wearing combat gear and carrying a weapon smashed the front window, forcing his way into the school. The school principal and psychologist tried tackling him to protect the children. He shot them both dead.

Teachers and other staff members heard the shooting and reacted quickly. One teacher helped students escape through a window. Most teachers

A student at Sandy Hook holds a sign with pictures of the victims, some of whom were her friends.

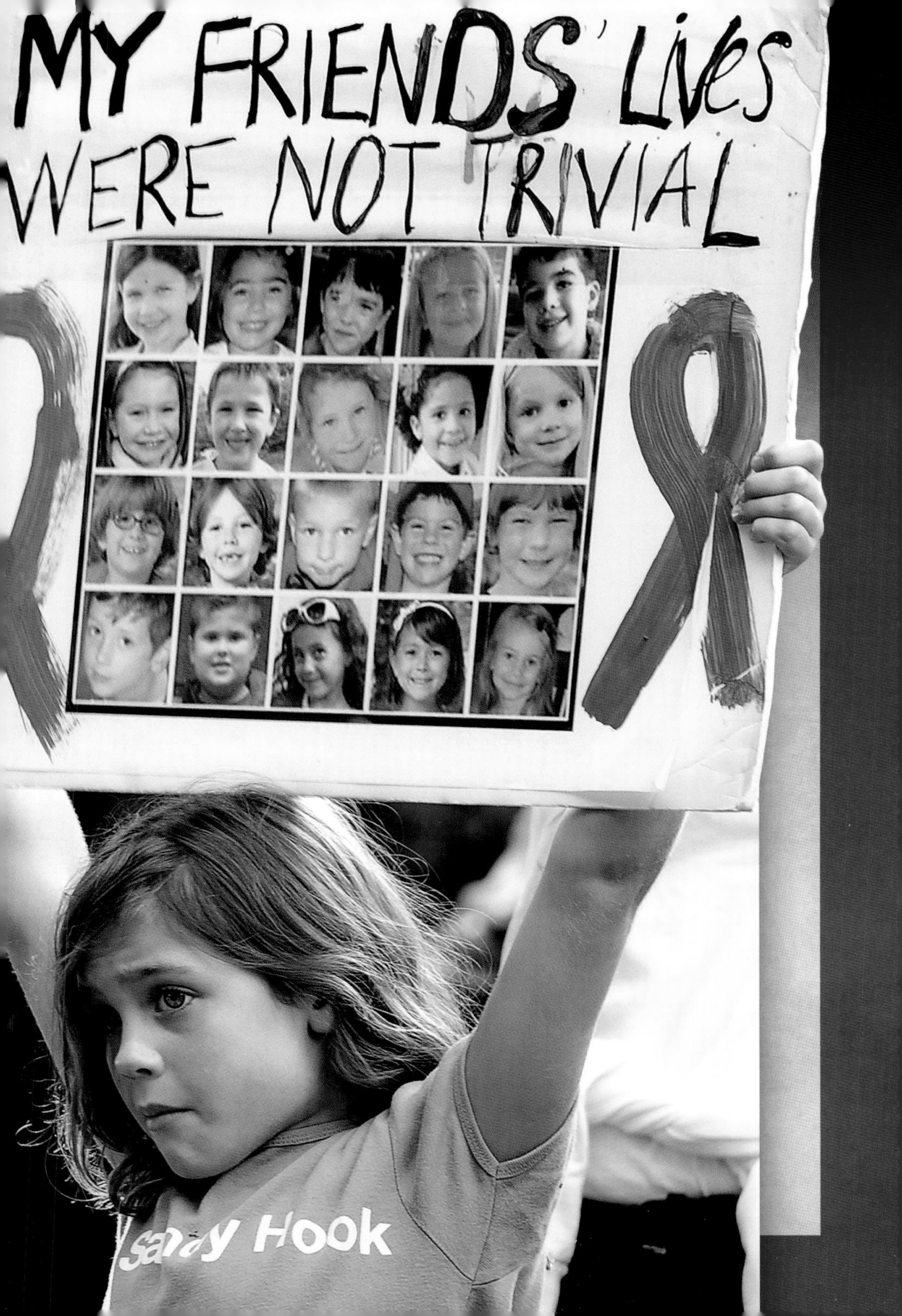
MY FRIENDS' LIVES
WERE NOT TRIVIAL
Sandy Hook

locked their classroom doors and closed the blinds. They herded students out of sight, into storage rooms or behind bookcases. They told the children to be quiet and protected them with their own bodies. But in two classrooms, this was not enough. Within five minutes, 20 first graders and four teachers lay dead. The gunman had shot them from close range, using a semiautomatic rifle. All victims were hit more than once and some at least 11 times. The gunman then shot and killed himself.

Twenty children, twelve girls and eight boys, were murdered at Sandy Hook that day. All were six or seven years old. Four teachers, the principal, and the school psychologist also died. Counting the shooter and his mother, whom he had killed earlier at home, 28 lives were lost on that December morning.[2] Newtown was changed forever.

WHY DID HE DO IT?

The shooter was Adam Lanza, age 20. He lived in Newtown with his mother, Nancy. Early that morning, he took his mother's guns, shot her, and drove to the school. Nancy, a gun enthusiast, legally owned five registered firearms.

Lanza used three in the massacre. These were a .223 Bushmaster semiautomatic rifle and two semiautomatic pistols. Lanza had easy access to guns and knew how to use them. Nancy had taken him to shooting ranges and taught him to shoot. The two even took gun safety courses offered by the National Rifle Association (NRA).

Nearly one year after the Sandy Hook shootings, investigators released a report summarizing Lanza's behavior before the massacre. According to the report, Lanza was highly interested in mass murders and had compiled a detailed spreadsheet of recent school shootings. He kept photocopies of newspaper articles about shootings of children dating back to 1891. He seemed particularly fascinated with the 1999 shootings at Colorado's Columbine High School. Games found at his home

GUN LAW CHANGES

In 2012, Connecticut required anyone buying a handgun to obtain a permit. A person had to undergo a criminal background check, pass a safety course, and be at least 21 years old. Connecticut did not require a permit for long guns, and the state generally did not regulate the sale or possession of ammunition. In April 2013, Connecticut strengthened its gun laws to require background checks for all gun and ammunition purchases. It also set a minimum age of 18 for possession of a long gun, limited the ability of mentally ill people to buy guns, and expanded the state's ban on assault weapons to include more than 100 additional firearms, including the semiautomatic rifle used by Lanza.

included many with violent content. In one, called School Shooting, the player controls a character who carries out a school shooting.

The Sandy Hook report concluded Lanza acted alone and that he carefully planned the attack, including his suicide. But the report did not explain why he attacked the school and murdered children and teachers. We may never know Lanza's motives, despite the extensive information collected on him.

THE IMMEDIATE RESPONSE

Immediately after the shooting, people called for changes, including better state and federal gun laws, better school security, and more attention to mental health. People across the country called for conversations to figure out how to prevent such a tragedy from happening again. Some schools increased their security by requiring all visitors to check in and adding more surveillance equipment, secure entries, and fencing. Some

"I PROMISE TO DO ALL I CAN TO PROTECT CHILDREN FROM GUN VIOLENCE BY ENCOURAGING AND SUPPORTING SOLUTIONS THAT CREATE SAFER, HEALTHIER HOMES, SCHOOLS AND COMMUNITIES."[3]

—THE SANDY HOOK PROMISE, MADE BY EACH OF THE ORGANIZATION'S MEMBERS

Demonstrators marched through Manhattan, New York, on January 21, 2012, calling for stricter gun laws.

school districts added an armed police officer at each school. Although many education groups think only police officers should carry guns in schools, some schools began arming teachers.

During the year following the Newtown tragedy, legislators in various states proposed more than 450 bills and resolutions, but only 108 became law. Forty-three of these were related to school emergency planning, such as requiring school districts to practice lockdown drills or forming study groups on school safety.[4]

Two US senators, Joe Manchin (D-WV) and Pat Toomey (R-PA), attempted to expand background checks on potential gun buyers. Their amendment to the Safe Communities, Safe Schools Act of 2013 would have added background checks for online and gun show purchases but not for transfers between family and friends. This would have partially closed the loophole that makes it possible for anyone—including criminals, drug users, and the mentally ill—to buy a gun without a background check.

Current federal law requires background checks only on people buying guns from licensed gun dealers. But guns can be purchased online, at gun shows from unlicensed dealers, or from any private person without a background check, or in some cases, before the check is complete. Up to 40 percent of gun sales are private and undocumented.[5] Despite overwhelming public support for background checks for all gun purchases—91 percent in a Gallup poll taken in January 2013—the Manchin-Toomey amendment was defeated in the Senate.[6]

NEWTOWN REACTS

Parents, friends, and family of the Sandy Hook victims quickly united to fight gun violence. The Newtown Action Alliance advocates for safer and smarter gun laws and cultural changes. It builds cooperation among groups impacted by gun violence and works to change the country's culture of gun violence. Sandy Hook Promise lobbies the government for stricter gun legislation.

THE LARGER PICTURE

Sandy Hook drew national attention to the problem of gun violence in the United States, and political and social leaders quickly spoke out. But the tragedy at Sandy Hook is in many ways unrepresentative of the overall problem. School shootings occur approximately once a month in the United States, and mass shootings occur approximately every two weeks.[7] But deaths from mass gun violence are statistically rare, and they are only the tip of the iceberg. Mass shootings account for less than 2 percent of annual gun deaths.[8] People are dying from gunshots not only in schools, but also in their homes, on the streets, and in churches, movie theaters, and workplaces.

Many Americans worry more about terrorism than gun violence. But between 2005 and 2015, only 71 Americans died in terrorist attacks on US soil, while 301,797 died from gun violence.[9] According to the Brady Campaign to Prevent Gun Violence, in an average year in the United States, 108,476 people are shot and 32,514 of them die. These shootings include murders, assaults, unintentional shootings, police shootings, and suicides and suicide attempts. Of those shot, 17,499 are below the age of 20, and 2,677 of these kids die.[10]

Why does it seem so little is being done to stop gun violence? One reason might be because the connection between gun control and the Second Amendment is not always clear. There are two questions to consider with regard to gun control: What does the Second Amendment

WHAT ARE BACKGROUND CHECKS?

Every person buying a gun through a federally licensed firearms dealer must complete a background check. It includes 16 questions covering their criminal and mental health history, dishonorable military discharges, immigration status, drug use, and whether they are under indictment for a crime. The gun dealer sends the answers and the person's social security number online or by telephone to the National Instant Criminal Background Check System (NICS) at the Federal Bureau of Investigation (FBI). Most denials are based on criminal convictions, with very few people denied for mental health reasons. Some states also run their own background checks.

protect? And what kinds of gun control make good policy sense?

Second Amendment supporters are committed to an individual's right to bear arms, and many of them oppose gun control. For some, the issue is simple: "Guns don't kill people; people kill people."[11] Occasionally, this gun rights talk emphasizes the right to bear arms with no consideration of individual responsibility.

Others have a different view of what the Second Amendment protects. They are more concerned with using legislation to develop sensible gun control measures that will save lives. The failure of these two sides to reach any agreement or compromise has often resulted in deadlocked legislatures, particularly at the national level. But Sandy Hook awakened in many people a new determination to find answers.

"IT IS NOT DISRESPECTFUL TO THE VICTIMS OF A TRAGEDY TO DISCUSS POSSIBLE WAYS THAT WE MIGHT AVOID SIMILAR TRAGEDIES."[12]

—DAVID KYLE JOHNSON, PHD, *PSYCHOLOGY TODAY*

CHAPTER TWO

THE SECOND
AMENDMENT

G un control is a matter of public policy, which can be decided at the local, state, or federal level. It takes the form of laws or regulations made on behalf of the public to solve a specific problem. But the US Constitution—and, specifically, the Bill of Rights— limits the kinds of laws and regulations the government can pass. It does this to protect rights and freedoms against political opinion. For example, the First Amendment protects the freedom of speech, including unpopular speech that many people might prefer to ban. What the Constitution permits, and what people might prefer as a matter of public policy, are not always the same thing.

Protestors gather outside the capitol in Albany, New York, in 2013 after tougher gun laws were introduced following the Sandy Hook massacre.

FREE
THE SEC
EPEAL
THE
E ACT
GUN OWNERS NEED TO "COMPROMISE"?
1934 - NATIONAL FIREARMS ACT
1968 - THE GUN CONTROL ACT
1986 - FIREARM OWNERS PROTECTION ACT
1993 - BRADY HANDGUN VIOLENCE ACT
1994 - "ASSAULT WEAPONS" BAN
1995 - GUN FREE SCHOOL ZONES ACT
WE HAVE COMPROMISED ENOUGH!
NO MORE INFRINGEMENTS!

The major constitutional restriction on gun control comes from the Second Amendment. It confers the right to bear arms. The text of the Second Amendment reads: "A well regulated Militia, being necessary to the security of a free State, the right of the people to keep and bear Arms, shall not be infringed."[1] The Bill of Rights, or the first ten amendments to the Constitution, was passed by Congress on September 25, 1789, and ratified by the states on December 15, 1791.

CONTEXT OF THE SECOND AMENDMENT

The Constitution was written from the point of view of life and politics in the late 1700s. Its framers could not foresee the many changes that would occur in the future. Thus, people today still constantly debate the meaning of every part

TODAY'S INTERPRETATIONS OF THE SECOND AMENDMENT

People interpret the Second Amendment in one of two ways: it confers either a militia right or an individual right. Those favoring stricter gun control believe it is a collective right, based on the first half of the Second Amendment. They believe the phrase "well regulated militia" makes regulation an integral part of the Second Amendment. Those favoring gun rights with little or no gun control concentrate on the second half of the Second Amendment, "the right of the people to keep and bear arms."[2] They see this as an individual right. The Supreme Court, in a divided decision in *District of Columbia v. Heller*, ruled in favor of the individual rights view, but specified some regulation is still allowed.

of the Constitution. The Second Amendment provokes passionate debates.

The Founding Fathers were divided into two groups. Anti-Federalists favored stronger states' rights and feared oppression from a centralized federal government. They demanded a Bill of Rights to protect individual liberties. They favored a part-time militia consisting of ordinary citizens instead of a standing army, which they feared would make it easier for the government to rise up against its citizens. Federalists favored a strong central government, which would control a well-armed, well-trained, full-time army.

Many anti-Federalists came to accept the necessity of a standing army, provided the Constitution also included a strong Bill of Rights to protect citizens' liberties, including the right to bear arms. Both concepts are implicit in the wording of the Constitution. The raising of armies is covered in Article I and the right to bear arms in the Second Amendment.

MINUTEMEN

Minutemen were an elite military force handpicked from the colonial militia. They were age 25 or younger, reliable, strong, and determined to defend the colonies. Minutemen were first mustered in Massachusetts in 1645. They fought American Indians and participated in the French and Indian War (1754–1763). The modern descendant of this early militia is the Army National Guard. During World War II (1939–1945), the government used the Minuteman symbol to encourage public participation and sacrifice for the war effort. Today, gun rights activists have adopted it to represent their attitudes, which emphasize individualism.

USE OF GUNS THEN AND NOW

Since 1791, the US military has grown into a vast, powerful structure. No one thinks state militias could defeat it. But this now seems unimportant because few people fear the US military would turn against its own citizens.

Henry Blodget, writing for *Business Insider*, points out ways our lives have changed since 1791. Then, the population was only 3.9 million people.[3] In 2016, the population was 323 million.[4] Slavery was still legal. There were only 13 states, all on the East Coast. With 1700s transportation technology, it took months to cross the country. There were still occasional conflicts with American Indians, and people hunted much of their own food. There were no police forces; people had to protect themselves. Thus, weapons were a necessity. But the typical gun was a single-shot musket that had to be manually reloaded before each shot. Given these differences, Blodget asks of the Second Amendment, "Can we all at least agree that it's a bit, if nothing else, outdated?"[5]

Now individuals own guns for different reasons. Civilians do not expect to be part of a militia. A 2013 survey revealed 48 percent of gun owners now consider protection the primary reason for owning a gun; 39 percent cited hunting or target shooting.[6] Other people collect guns.

Until assault weapons became popular, guns owned by civilians were typically very different from those used by the military. In the 1980s, Beretta developed a 9 mm high-capacity semiautomatic pistol. Beretta's goal was to make a military gun and then greatly increase its profits by

GUNS THEN AND NOW

The typical weapon in 1791 was the flintlock musket. Its long, smooth barrel was packed with gunpowder, with a ramrod used to push musket balls into place. A flintlock mechanism lit the gunpowder. When the trigger was pulled, a tiny piece of flint rubbed against the steel of the musket barrel, causing a spark. When the spark touched the gunpowder, the shot was fired. The musket was reloaded after every shot. The Bushmaster M4-type carbine is the assault rifle used by Lanza at Sandy Hook Elementary School. It is a more compact, civilian version of the military AR-15, or M16 rifle. It is typically capable of firing 30 times before reloading. Rounds fire at speeds almost three times the speed of sound.

Hunting is a popular reason why many people own guns.

selling it to the US public. Vietnam-era military assault rifles were legal until the 1994 Assault Weapons Ban (AWB). This ban expired in 2004.

WHAT DID THE FOUNDING FATHERS REALLY MEAN?

Even legal experts differ on their interpretation of the meaning of the Second Amendment. Two of these are Professor Nelson Lund of the George Mason University School of Law and Professor Adam Winkler of the UCLA School of Law.

Professor Lund compares the right to bear arms to freedom of speech, a part of the First Amendment. He argues that a person is not free to engage in damaging speech such as perjury or fraud. Likewise, "no reasonable person could believe that violent criminals should have unrestricted access to guns, or that any individual should possess a nuclear weapon."[7] Lund argues courts can restrict the use of arms to maintain an orderly society but cannot infringe on the right of citizens to protect themselves. He states that "most gun control laws can be viewed as efforts to save lives and prevent crime, which are perfectly reasonable goals."[8] However, he says, if those goals are used to justify infringements on individual liberty, the constitutional right to bear arms becomes meaningless.

Professor Winkler argues the phrase "well regulated militia" means gun control, as well as the right to bear arms, is an inherent part of the Second Amendment. He says, "While the Founders sought to protect the citizenry from being disarmed entirely, they did not wish to prevent government from adopting reasonable regulations of guns and gun owners."[9] He notes that many gun laws existed during the Founding era, and people did not consider the Second

"[THE SECOND AMENDMENT] HAS BEEN THE SUBJECT OF ONE OF THE GREATEST PIECES OF FRAUD, I REPEAT THE WORD 'FRAUD,' ON THE AMERICAN PUBLIC BY SPECIAL INTEREST GROUPS THAT I HAVE EVER SEEN IN MY LIFETIME."[10]

—FORMER SUPREME COURT CHIEF JUSTICE WARREN BURGER, DECEMBER 16, 1991

Amendment a "libertarian license for anyone to have any kind of ordinary firearm, anywhere they wanted."[11] It did not protect the right to revolt against the government. It was meant to ensure public safety.

Unlike Lund, Winkler does not consider it reasonable to compare the First and Second Amendments. The Second Amendment specifically recognizes that the armed citizenry must be "well regulated."[12] Winkler believes the regulation of gun control is built into the Second Amendment. He thinks the Second Amendment aligns better with the Fourth Amendment, which protects the right to privacy but also authorizes the government to conduct "reasonable searches and seizures."[13] In both cases, the protected rights are limited.

COURT CASES

The Supreme Court has ruled on several Second Amendment cases. The two most relevant cases have been decided since 2000. In the 2008 case of *District of Columbia v. Heller*, the court ruled that a ban on handguns in Washington, DC, was unconstitutional. This was the first Supreme Court decision that specifically interpreted the Second Amendment as protecting the individual right to bear arms, as opposed to the use of arms in militia service. The judgment applied only to federal areas, such as Washington, DC, not to the states. Nevertheless, it was seen as a blow to gun control advocates.

"IN SUM, WE HOLD THAT THE DISTRICT'S BAN ON HANDGUN POSSESSION IN THE HOME VIOLATES THE SECOND AMENDMENT, AS DOES ITS PROHIBITION AGAINST RENDERING ANY LAWFUL FIREARM IN THE HOME OPERABLE FOR THE PURPOSE OF IMMEDIATE SELF-DEFENSE."[15]

—JUSTICE ANTONIN SCALIA, SUPREME COURT, *DISTRICT OF COLUMBIA V. HELLER*, 2008

The 2010 *McDonald v. Chicago* decision extended this individual right to the states. However, the court was careful to say the right is subject to reasonable regulation. It reads in part, "The Court's opinion should not be taken to cast doubt on long-standing prohibitions on the possession of firearms by felons and the mentally ill, or laws forbidding the carrying of firearms in sensitive places such as schools and government buildings, or laws imposing conditions and qualifications on the commercial sale of arms."[14]

CHAPTER THREE

A SHORT
HISTORY OF
GUN CONTROL

G un control is not a recent development. By some measures, governments controlled guns much more strictly during colonial times than they do today. In 1619, Virginia made it illegal to transfer guns to American Indians. Breaking this law was punishable by death. Laws in other colonies prohibited giving or selling arms to various groups of people, including slaves and servants.

Legal scholar Winkler points out that, in early America, guns were "private property with a public purpose."[1] Militias used them to defend the

Minutemen in Massachusetts grab their weapons before heading out to fight in the Battle of Lexington.

government. The Uniform Militia Act of 1792 required able-bodied white males under the age of 45 to arm themselves and gather or assemble with a local militia. States and towns regulated gunpowder storage. In many places, it was illegal to discharge weapons within city limits or carry a loaded weapon to a gathering. Governments could confiscate guns or hold them in central locations for local defense. During the late 1700s and early 1800s, both state and federal governments went door-to-door, asking people how many guns they had and whether the guns were functional.

In the early 1800s, many states banned the concealed carrying of firearms to limit dueling and vengeful acts. Some states passed laws preventing concealed weapons unless the person had reason to feel threatened. Such laws were passed throughout the states and territories.

CHANGES IN THE 1900s

"WHILE GUN POSSESSION IS AS OLD AS THE COUNTRY, SO IS GUN REGULATION."[2]

—ROBERT J. SPITZER, STATE UNIVERSITY OF NEW YORK COLLEGE AT CORTLAND

Despite state and local laws, the Second Amendment remained relatively undiscussed in the courts for more than 150 years.

New gun laws in the 1800s were meant to limit or stop duels that had become common in the Wild West.

Winkler notes that, before 1959, very few articles on the Second Amendment were published in law journals, and none argued in favor of an individual's right to bear arms. Then, between 1980 and 1999, there were 125 law review articles on the Second Amendment, most supporting the individual-rights viewpoint. Individual-rights supporters began to describe their viewpoint as the "standard model" of Second Amendment interpretation, and the name stuck, despite its short history.[3]

Also, despite gun laws, it became extremely easy to obtain firearms. Guns are sold at chain stores and family shops. A background check takes only minutes, and less than 1 percent of requests are denied.[4] A person who fails a background check can easily obtain a gun through the Internet, from a friend or family member, or at a gun show. Notorious events throughout the 1900s caused many people to question the wisdom of nearly unrestricted gun access and led to calls for stricter national gun control. But attempts to strengthen gun regulations result in strong pushbacks from gun rights advocates. Most gun regulation still occurs at the state and local levels, and laws vary greatly from state to state.

LAWS IN THE 1900s

The National Firearms Act of 1934 was one of the first major federal attempts at gun control. It was passed in response to the rise in gangster violence in the 1920s and 1930s. It targeted fully automatic weapons, short-barreled shotguns and rifles, and pen and cane guns. The Federal Firearms Act of 1938 added a requirement that anyone selling or shipping firearms must be licensed by the

US Department of Commerce. This prohibited the sale of guns to people convicted of certain crimes and required the seller to log the buyer's name and address.

After the 1963 assassination of President John F. Kennedy, Congress did not tighten gun regulations. The Gun Control Act of 1968 was spurred by the assassination of Martin Luther King Jr. in April, followed by that of Robert F. Kennedy two months later. The new law prohibited the mail-order sale of rifles and shotguns and increased licensing requirements for gun sellers. It added convicted felons, drug users, and the mentally incompetent to the list of people barred from owning firearms. But an anti–gun control campaign by the NRA delayed its passage. This greatly frustrated President Lyndon B. Johnson, who stated at the bill's signing,

TYPES OF GUNS

There are two basic types of guns: handguns and long guns. A handgun, such as a pistol or revolver, is a firearm designed to be held and fired by a single hand. A long gun, such as a rifle or shotgun, has a longer barrel and is typically fired braced against the shooter's shoulder. A semiautomatic firearm is self-loading but will fire only one round each time the trigger is pulled. An automatic weapon, sometimes called a machine gun, is capable of firing more than one round on a single pull of the trigger. Assault firearms are semiautomatic weapons that look like military weapons and have features such as folding stocks, pistol grips, bayonet mounts, or flash suppressors.

"IF GUNS ARE TO BE KEPT OUT OF THE HANDS OF THE CRIMINAL, OUT OF THE HANDS OF THE INSANE, AND OUT OF THE HANDS OF THE IRRESPONSIBLE, THEN WE MUST HAVE LICENSING."[6]

—PRESIDENT LYNDON B. JOHNSON, OCTOBER 1968, AT THE SIGNING OF THE GUN CONTROL ACT

"The voices that blocked these safeguards were not the voices of an aroused nation. They were the voices of a powerful lobby, a gun lobby."[5]

After the attempted assassination of President Ronald Reagan in 1981, which also wounded a police officer, a secret service agent, and Press Secretary James Brady, it was 12 years before changes were made. Two laws were passed. The Brady Handgun Violence Prevention Act, known as "the Brady Bill," signed by President Bill Clinton in 1993, required a five-day waiting period and a background check before the purchase of a handgun. This bill also set up the NICS. The Violent Crime Control and Law Enforcement Act of 1994, or AWB, banned many assault weapons. This law was designed to last for ten years, after which it would have to be reauthorized by Congress. In 2004, Congress allowed the law to expire.

GUN CONTROL APPROACHES AFTER 2000

In the 2000s, state and federal laws allow people to buy and possess firearms. But other laws regulate this right. Gun control laws vary by state and by their degree of restriction. Rural areas tend to have more lenient laws; urban areas with high crime rates tend to be more restrictive. Utah, Alaska, and Arizona, plus several southern and western states, have the least restrictive gun laws. California, Connecticut, and New Jersey have the most restrictive laws.

Forms of gun control also vary. Some states require gun owners to obtain permits and register their guns. A few states require potential gun purchasers to complete a gun safety course. Other common types of gun control include waiting periods and background checks. A waiting

JAMES BRADY AND GUN CONTROL

James Brady was President Reagan's press secretary. On March 30, 1981, John Hinckley Jr., who had a history of mental problems and stalking, shot and injured Reagan, Brady, and two other people. Using a .22-caliber revolver, Hinckley fired six shots within two to three seconds. The first shot hit Brady in the head, partially paralyzing him. The shooting led Brady and his wife, Sarah, to work to keep guns from dangerous people. They founded the Brady Campaign to Prevent Gun Violence and tirelessly lobbied Congress to pass gun control legislation. Finally, in 1993, President Clinton signed the Brady Handgun Violence Prevention Act.

NRA instructor Bob Frankenfield supervises Marianne Hudson as she takes part in a gun safety course, which is a prerequisite for a concealed weapon license in Florida.

period is the time between purchasing a gun and being allowed to take possession of it. Waiting periods are meant to reduce impulsive, violent gun use. Background checks are designed to prevent potentially dangerous people from obtaining weapons. Certain categories of people are prohibited from possessing firearms, including convicted felons, fugitives, drug addicts, domestic abusers, undocumented immigrants, and people with certain kinds of mental health histories.

Other forms of gun control relate to the types of guns that can be sold. Fully automatic weapons and short-barrel firearms have been heavily regulated since the 1934 National Firearms Act. In addition, certain assault weapons are banned in some states. Gun control laws change in response to current events, including mass shootings, and in response to the ongoing gun control debate. In the late 2000s, for example, there were many discussions and changes to laws regarding concealed carrying of firearms and the presence of guns in school zones.

The main progun lobby remains the NRA. Even more conservative groups, such as the National Association for Gun Rights, are also growing. But new pro–gun control organizations are rising to oppose these groups. The debate between individual gun rights and gun control advocates is still going strong.

PRO—GUN CONTROL GROUPS

In the last few decades, pro–gun control groups have shown new energy, in part because of the rise of gun violence. The Coalition to Stop Gun Violence, founded in 1974, is a coalition of 47 social justice, religious, public health, and child welfare organizations.[7] Former New York City mayor Michael Bloomberg organized Everytown for Gun Safety. It is a coalition of three groups: Moms Demand Action for Gun Sense in America, Mayors against Illegal Guns, and survivors of gun violence.

CHAPTER FOUR

THE RISE OF
THE NRA

The recent history of gun control in the United States can be understood only by following the rise of the NRA. Two former members of the Union army, Colonel William C. Church and General George Wingate, founded the NRA on November 17, 1871. They were "dismayed that so many Northern soldiers, often poorly trained, had been scarcely capable of using their weapons."[1] They wanted to promote rifle shooting by setting up an organization to train shooters. The NRA's first president was Ambrose Burnside, a Union army general. This choice of president reflected the understanding of the Second Amendment at that time—the need to have a prepared citizen militia

General Ambrose Burnside served as governor of Rhode Island and as a US senator before becoming president of the NRA.

capable of assisting the government in domestic military matters, such as raids or invasions.

The NRA's first goal was developing a rifle practice range on a farm on Long Island, New York. The group held shooting matches every summer. In 1903, NRA Secretary Albert S. Jones began promoting the establishment of rifle clubs at colleges, universities, and military academies. The NRA's focus for its first century was displayed at its national headquarters, now in Fairfax, Virginia: "Firearms Safety Education, Marksmanship Training, Shooting for Recreation."[2] NRA youth programs still sponsor rifle training for more than one million youth.

THE PRO-GUN CONTROL NRA

For a century, the NRA favored reasonable gun control measures. The 1920s and 1930s saw the rise of big-city gangsters using weapons such as sawed-off shotguns and machine guns. President Franklin D. Roosevelt made gun control and crime fighting part of his New Deal, a series of programs designed to help Americans overcome the effects of the Great Depression of the 1930s. The NRA helped write the federal gun control legislation that

Women and children were encouraged to participate in rifle training at the NRA practice range.

became the National Firearms Act of 1934 and the Federal Firearms Act of 1938.

During this time, state gun regulations were not controversial. The National Revolver Association, the NRA branch involved in handgun training, proposed gun legislation for states. It supported requiring a permit to carry a concealed weapon, adding five years to a sentence if a gun was used in a crime, and preventing noncitizens from owning handguns. They also supported two measures the NRA now opposes—a one-day waiting period between buying and receiving a gun and requiring gun dealers to turn over sales records to police. Nine states approved the NRA's suggested legislation. Nine others approved it with a two-day waiting period.[3]

As late as 1963, after the Kennedy assassination, the NRA still supported gun control to maintain public safety. Assassin Lee Harvey Oswald bought his weapon through a mail-order ad in *American Rifleman*, the NRA magazine. The NRA vice president, testifying before Congress, supported a ban on mail-order gun sales. However, no new laws were passed.

"I HAVE NEVER BELIEVED IN THE GENERAL PRACTICE OF CARRYING WEAPONS. . . . I DO NOT BELIEVE IN THE GENERAL PROMISCUOUS TOTING OF GUNS. I THINK IT SHOULD BE SHARPLY RESTRICTED AND ONLY UNDER LICENSES."[5]

—KARL T. FREDERICK, NRA PRESIDENT, 1934

Race riots during the 1960s inflamed fear in white lawmakers over militant civil rights groups having access to guns. In 1967, a group of Black Panther Party members entered the California Statehouse carrying rifles to protest a gun control bill. California Governor Ronald Reagan stated, "There's no reason why on the street today a citizen should be carrying loaded weapons."[4] These fears plus the back-to-back assassinations of Martin Luther King Jr. and Robert F. Kennedy spurred passage of the Gun Control Act of 1968. But the NRA blocked the two strongest proposals in the original bill—a national gun registry and mandatory licenses for all gun owners. They considered these actions too restrictive.

THE REVOLT AT CINCINNATI

NRA leaders in 1977 were still focused on hunting and marksmanship. But there were rebels within the organization. They wanted a political organization that would fight all attempts at gun control. They staged the Revolt at Cincinnati at the annual NRA convention on May 21, 1977. They succeeded overwhelmingly. As rebel John D. Aquilino put it, "Before Cincinnati, you had a bunch of people who wanted to turn the NRA into a sports publishing organization and get rid of guns."[6] After Cincinnati, the NRA became a grassroots lobbying organization bent on stopping all gun control legislation. It closely associated itself with the Republican Party.

The architects of this change included Neal Knox and Harlon Carter. Both men believed gun control laws threatened basic US freedoms and would lead to disarmament of the country's citizens. Knox even

Harlon Carter, *left*, and Neal Knox, *right*, turned the NRA into a more politically minded organization.

suggested the 1960s assassinations might have been plots designed to lead to gun control and disarmament. Carter, already an NRA board member, had founded the group's Institute for Legislative Action (ILA) in 1975. By the end of the Cincinnati Revolt, Carter was executive vice president of the NRA. He replaced the old NRA motto on its Washington, DC, headquarters with the second half of the Second Amendment: "The Right of the People to Keep and Bear Arms Shall Not Be Infringed."[7] The NRA had become a political action group. It has never looked back.

THE NRA TODAY

After the Revolt at Cincinnati, the NRA expanded both its contributions to political campaigns and its language regarding the Second Amendment. Articles began appearing in *American Rifleman* supporting the view that the Second Amendment confers the individual right to bear arms. This view was not supported by most jurists of the time. But the US public and its elected leaders quickly came around, beginning with Utah Senator Orrin Hatch, who endorsed the idea in 1982.

An early NRA victory was the passage of the 1986 Firearm Owners' Protection Act. This legislation made interstate firearm sales easier and prevented the government from creating a gun-owner database. Some lawmakers wanted to vote against the bill but feared pushback from the NRA. The fight by gun control advocates passing the Brady Bill made the NRA push even harder against gun control laws. It also attracted many high-profile members, including actor Charlton Heston, who was NRA president from 1998 through 2003.

The NRA has not lost a fight over federal gun control legislation since the assault-weapons ban in 1994—which was not renewed in 2004. It helps shape all federal gun legislation and continues to be highly vocal regarding gun rights. The NRA supported background checks as recently as 1999, but NRA executive vice president Wayne LaPierre now says they do not work. Congress follows the lead of the NRA. Thus, despite overwhelming public support for universal background checks for all gun sales, this simple form of gun control had still not become law nationwide in 2016.

The NRA's influence is extremely strong at the state level. It works tirelessly in every state to decrease or eliminate firearm regulations. It works to prevent lawsuits against the gun industry and against shooting ranges and to eliminate restrictions on guns in public places such as bars and campuses. It also works closely with the gun industry.

However, according to Winkler, "The National Rifle Association's days of being a political powerhouse may be numbered."[9] Winkler points out that most NRA supporters are white, rural, and less educated. But combined minority groups, including African Americans, Hispanics, and Asian Americans, will soon outnumber whites.

WAYNE LAPIERRE— VOICE OF THE NRA

Neal Knox appointed Wayne LaPierre an NRA lobbyist in 1978. Since 1991, LaPierre has been the NRA's executive vice president. He is known for his confrontational style and controversial anti-gun control statements. He sees any gun control as an unacceptable loss of freedom. After passage of the assault-weapons ban in 1994, he said the ban "gives jackbooted Government thugs more power to take away our constitutional rights, break in our doors, seize our guns, destroy our property and even injure and kill us."[10] This extreme statement led some high-profile members, including former president George H. W. Bush, to resign from the NRA.

These groups tend to favor gun control. In addition, most people are now urban dwellers, who strongly favor gun control. Thus, simply as a consequence of the changing mix of groups in the country, Winkler says, support for the gun rights position of the NRA is likely to decline in the coming years.

FROM THE
HEADLINES

TRAYVON MARTIN AND THE STAND YOUR GROUND LAW

On the evening of February 26, 2012, 17-year-old Trayvon Martin bought a bag of Skittles and a can of iced tea at a convenience store. Walking home, he encountered George Zimmerman, a neighborhood watch volunteer. Zimmerman had just called 911, saying he was watching a suspicious guy who looked like he wasn't up to good. The suspicious guy was Martin.

No one saw what happened next, but several people heard screams of "Help, help!" followed by a gunshot.[11] When police arrived, Martin was facedown on the ground, dying, with a bullet in his chest. Zimmerman was standing over him, holding his 9 mm semiautomatic handgun. He had a facial injury. Zimmerman claimed Martin had attacked him, and he shot in self-defense. He was not arrested.

The shooting triggered protests around the country. Many people thought Martin was targeted because he was African American. Zimmerman was eventually charged with second-degree murder, but a jury found him not guilty. Florida's "stand your ground" law makes it easy to plead self-defense, as Zimmerman did. The law, passed in 2005, allows citizens to use deadly force when they feel threatened.

Protestors marched in Florida in memory of Trayvon Martin after he was killed.

CHAPTER FIVE

REASONS FOR
GUN CONTROL

T ypes of gun control vary considerably. They range from rules regarding safe storage of guns and ammunition, to background checks and registration, to the complete banning of some or all assault weapons. Most people favor some form of gun control, although they disagree on how much and what kind of regulation is best. Others are strongly opposed to any gun control. But what reasons lie behind these positions? Most reasons in favor of gun control are based on practical or societal factors, statistics, or, in some cases, individual philosophies.

People gathered after the Virginia Tech shooting to support closing a loophole allowing criminals and the mentally ill to buy firearms at gun shows without a background check.

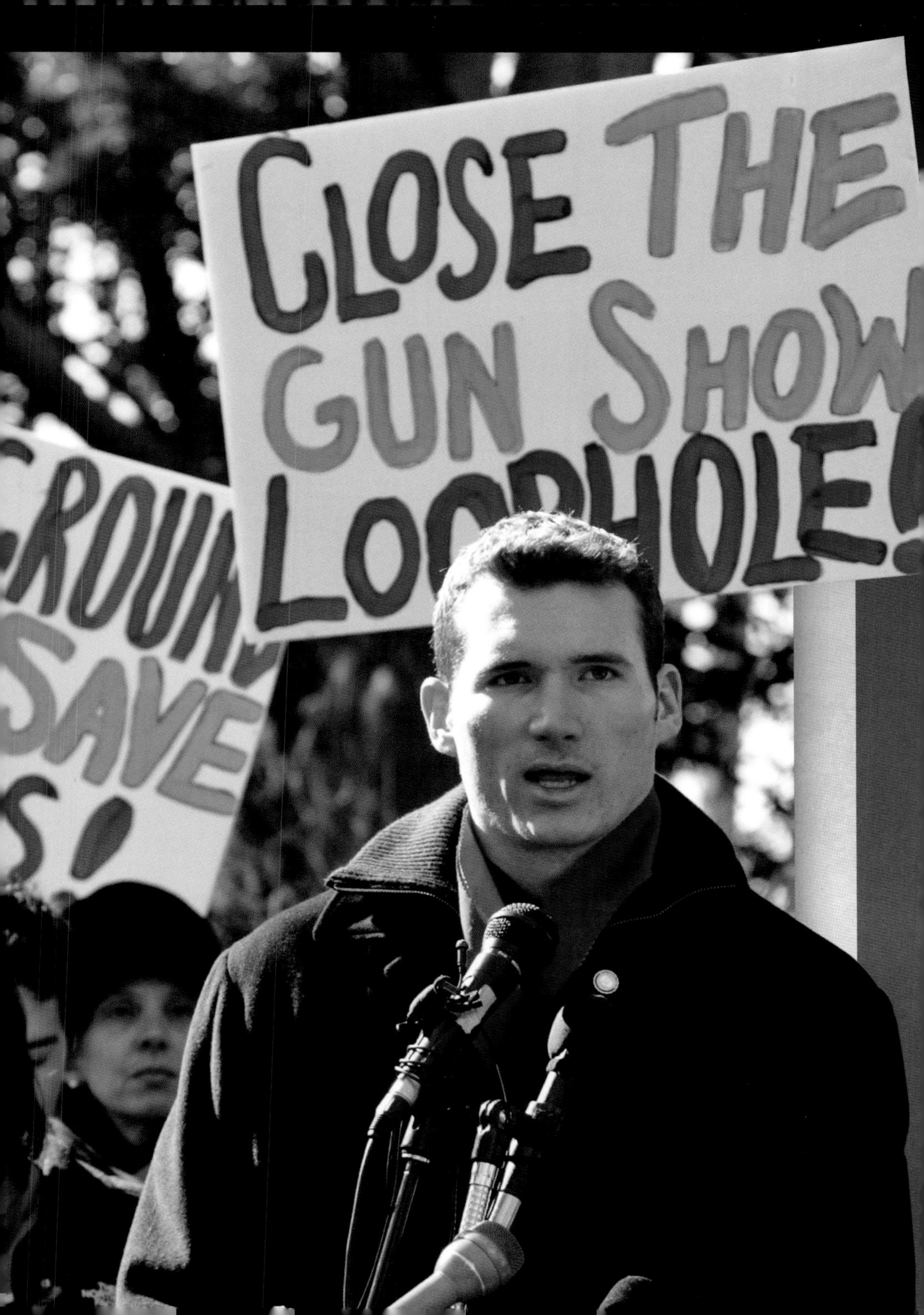
CLOSE THE
GUN SHOW
LOOPHOLE!

COMMONSENSE GUN REGULATIONS

The uses of guns in society have changed profoundly since the Constitution was written. Forty-eight percent of legal gun owners in the United States now use guns for personal protection, and another 39 percent for hunting or target shooting. These numbers have changed recently; as late as 1999, only 26 percent considered protection their primary reason for gun ownership.[1]

A 2013 survey showed most Americans support "commonsense" gun laws. Eighty-three percent support universal background checks. Fifty-six percent favor banning assault weapons and 53 percent favor high-capacity magazine bans. Ninety percent approve of preventing the mentally ill from purchasing guns, and 60 percent approve of a federal database tracking gun sales.[2] As of 2016, there was no national firearms registry. The Firearm Owners' Protection Act of 1986 makes it illegal to keep such a database. Although the 1993 Brady Bill created a background check system for sales by licensed gun dealers, the records for each background check must be destroyed within 24 hours.

SOCIAL REASONS FOR GUN CONTROL

The Harvard School of Public Health found that, generally, as the number of guns per individual increases, the homicide rate also increases. This was true in the United States and in 26 foreign countries. The same trend occurs with suicides. In addition, many gun-related deaths are accidental. Thus, a major reason for favoring gun control is to reduce gun deaths. Half of 62 mass shootings between 1982 and 2012 used high-capacity magazines. This raised death rates by 63 percent and injury rates by 156 percent. Many gang-related shootings involve magazines with a capacity of 30 to 90 rounds.[3] In mass shootings, inability to obtain high-capacity magazines would save lives.

HIGH-CAPACITY MAGAZINES

High-capacity magazines, those holding ten or more rounds of ammunition, are often used in mass shootings. Thus, many gun control advocates assume banning these magazines would decrease gun deaths. One useful piece of evidence for this comes from the federal assault weapons ban. The *Washington Post* tracked the number of high-capacity magazines seized from criminals during and after the ban. During the ban, the number declined steadily. After the ban expired, the numbers went up again. A gun expert had been skeptical the ban would work, but the data changed his mind.

GUN CONTROL AND EQUALITY

Jacob Schuman, a criminal defense attorney, offers an argument for gun control that counters the "right to bear arms" argument of gun rights advocates. He says widespread gun availability increases inequality by making life more violent and less stable in poor communities. Crime rates are higher and crime is more lethal in poor areas. Because poverty is much greater in minority communities, minorities suffer most from gun violence. Schuman says, "A young black man in Chicago, Illinois, has a 38,000 percent greater chance of being shot than a white person. This is a blatant form of racial inequality."[4] He sees this inequality as a potent argument in favor of gun control.

Others say stronger gun control would protect women from domestic abuse. When a gun is present during a domestic dispute, a woman is far more likely to be murdered. Also, legally obtained guns can be stolen and used by criminals. Thus, gun control advocates argue, when more legal guns are present in the population, more will likely be used to commit crimes. The societal costs of crime, in addition to loss of life, are very high. The World Health Organization lists the following as costs of gun violence: legal and medical costs; psychological costs; costs for policing, imprisonment, and control of criminals; life insurance; private security; foster care; decreased tourism; and lowered property values.

There are two more practical reasons why people advocate gun control. First, when a gun is readily available, arguments or brawls, as well as robberies and assaults, are much more likely to escalate, resulting in serious injury or death. Second, many people assume armed citizens will be able to stop mass shooters. But an armed civilian stopped none of the 62 mass shootings between 1982 and 2012.[5] Some people claim civilians stopped a 2002 shooting at Appalachian School of Law. However, current and former law enforcement officers, not civilians, stopped it after the shooter ran out of ammunition.

GUNS AND SELF-DEFENSE

How often do Americans use guns in self-defense? The best estimates come from the National Crime Victimization Survey (NCVS). They report that victims use a gun in approximately 1 percent of crimes of personal contact. This rises to 3 percent in home invasions. In 1995, there were 70,000 defensive gun uses (DGUs) in violent crimes. In 2010, there were 50,000. There were another 30,000 DGUs against burglars in both years.[6]

WHO NEEDS THEM?

One final argument of gun control advocates is more a matter of philosophy. This is the idea that civilians, including hunters, have no reason to own military types of guns and accessories such as the AR-15 rifle, a semiautomatic weapon that is the civilian version of the military's M16 rifle. Besides magazines that can fire up to

> "THE AVERAGE GUN OWNER, NO MATTER HOW RESPONSIBLE, IS NOT TRAINED IN LAW ENFORCEMENT OR ON HOW TO HANDLE LIFE-THREATENING SITUATIONS, SO IN MOST CASES, IF A THREAT OCCURS, INCREASING THE NUMBER OF GUNS ONLY CREATES A MORE VOLATILE AND DANGEROUS SITUATION."[8]
>
> **—PROFESSOR JEFFREY VOCCOLA, KUTZTOWN UNIVERSITY**

90 rounds before reloading, today's semiautomatic and automatic weapons include accessories that make killing much easier. These include silencers, flash suppressors, and gunstocks that telescope, fold, or detach. Such accessories help conceal the shooter's presence. Some weapons even include grenade launchers.

At one time, even gun rights advocates, including both the NRA and President Reagan, agreed there was no reason for civilians to own such weapons. The NRA supported the assault weapons ban of 1994, which banned many of these guns. But today, gun rights advocates, including many NRA members, hotly dispute any attempt to ban any guns, including fully automatic weapons.

Investigative reporter Robert Parry thinks Americans who favor the interpretation that the Second Amendment gives unrestricted gun rights have adopted a "false history" of the amendment.[7] These people think the framers intended to arm anarchists so they could rise up against the government if they disagreed with it. He states that, rather than giving individuals the right to bear arms against the country, the framers of the Bill of Rights intended the opposite. They wanted to establish state militias to maintain order and protect the government against uprisings. The real history, he says, shows the Second Amendment is a collective, not an individual, right.

NO FUNDING FOR GUN VIOLENCE RESEARCH

Lack of evidence to support or refute the value of various forms of gun control is partly due to passage of the 1997 Dickey Amendment, which stated, "none of the funds made available for injury prevention and control at the Centers for Disease Control and Prevention (CDC) may be used to advocate or promote gun control."[10] The NRA campaigned for this amendment after the CDC published a well-received research article in 1993 titled "Gun Ownership as a Risk Factor for Homicide in the Home." The paper concluded the presence of guns in the home correlated with an increased risk of homicide. The amendment did not explicitly ban research on gun violence, but it removed nearly all funding; thus, research has effectively been halted.

The Second Amendment describes gun ownership in the context of maintaining a "well regulated militia."[9] Very strict gun control laws were an accepted fact in the colonies and early states. Thus, people who favor gun control conclude the Second Amendment is not a legal obstacle to reasonable forms of gun control.

FROM THE HEADLINES

THE ORLANDO MASSACRE

In the early hours of June 12, 2016, the deadliest mass shooting in US history to that time occurred in an Orlando, Florida, gay nightclub called Pulse. Omar Mateen, a 29-year-old security guard, opened fire, killing 49 people and wounding 53 more.[11] He then held hostages for several hours before local SWAT teams burst in and killed him. Most of Mateen's victims were Hispanic and members of the LGBT community. Family members described Mateen as abusive and homophobic.

Mateen had three weapons, including an AR-15 assault-type rifle. He bought the weapons legally and passed a background check. He also passed background checks to become a security guard. He was placed on a terrorist watch list and investigated twice by the FBI, but the investigations were closed. Investigators described Mateen as a "homegrown terrorist."[12] Born in New York, he was strongly influenced by terrorist websites. In a 911 call during the shootings, he pledged allegiance to ISIS, the radical Middle Eastern terrorist group. He apparently acted alone.

Following the shooting, politicians made statements condemning the shooter and supporting the survivors. Republican Speaker Paul Ryan called for a moment of silence. However, he refused to consider several bills that had been introduced to curb gun violence. Several House Democrats angrily protested and left the House chamber.

Mourners console each other outside of Pulse nightclub.

CHAPTER SIX

REASONS
AGAINST GUN
CONTROL

S ome anti–gun control activists strongly believe the Second Amendment conveys an absolute right for individuals to own and use guns. They believe this means people have the right to own an unlimited number of guns of any kind. They are against all forms of gun control. Most people have more moderate views—they favor an individual's right to bear arms but also favor reasonable restrictions on this right. Again, the types of gun control they favor vary; those generally against gun control will tend to favor fewer restrictions and oppose laws that would ban weapons.

Gun owners tend to favor an individual's right to carry a firearm.

WHO ARE GUN RIGHTS ADVOCATES?

Philip J. Cook and Kristin A. Goss, authors of *The Gun Debate*, point out that most gun owners come from families with a long tradition of gun ownership. These families used guns for various purposes, including hunting and target practice. The idea of owning guns for self-protection is recent. Cook and Goss think it may relate to current discussion in the news of Second Amendment rights, which people associate with self-protection. It is not due to more crime. Crime rates have decreased since the 1990s.

This tradition of gun ownership results in a strong division between gun rights and gun control advocates. Gun owners are more likely than nonowners to be gun rights advocates. They are also

THE GUN RIGHTS MOVEMENT

Many groups work to protect and increase gun rights. National and state membership groups, including the NRA, carry out political activities and talk to the media. Think tanks and researchers, such as the Second Amendment Foundation, collect data and sponsor lawsuits to overturn gun control laws. Gun shops, sport shooting organizations, and safety and training organizations bring gun lovers together, keep people informed, and reinforce the gun rights message. The gun industry is not particularly politically active, but they are closely associated with the NRA. Political action committees raise money to support political candidates. Many individuals also challenge gun laws. A group of libertarian sheriffs have said they will refuse to enforce gun control laws they consider unconstitutional.

more likely to be suspicious of new gun control efforts. The groups also show strong divisions by political party, gender, and race. Gun rights advocates tend to be mostly Republican or Independent, male, and white; groups including Democrats, females, and blacks tend to be gun control supporters. Most people tend to support expanded background checks, but gun rights supporters, overall, are strongly opposed to most gun control.

LEGAL REASONS FOR GUN RIGHTS

A major reason given by those who oppose gun control relates to the legal and constitutional right to bear arms. They concentrate on the last half of the Second Amendment. The right to bear arms for nonmilitia purposes was not recognized for much of the nation's history. However, recent Supreme Court decisions in *District of Columbia*

WHO OWNS THE GUNS?

Approximately one-fourth of Americans own guns—37 percent of men and 12 percent of women.[1] Middle-aged white people are more likely, and young blacks less likely, to own guns; rural dwellers are more likely than urban dwellers. Higher incomes result in higher gun ownership. Gun ownership is highest in southern, midwestern, and old western frontier states. It is lowest in the Northeast, mid-Atlantic, and Pacific states, with the exceptions of Vermont and Alaska, where rates are high.

v. Heller (2008) and *McDonald v. City of Chicago* (2010) supported it.

Many people say stricter gun laws would make it more difficult to protect their homes and families. Most gun owners say they feel safer with a gun in the house. Others say gun control laws, particularly those banning assault weapons, infringe on the rights of hunters and target shooters. Shotguns and semiautomatic rifles, some less powerful than common hunting rifles, are used in shooting competitions. These are included in some assault weapons bans.

Other gun rights advocates object to specific gun control measures such as background checks and microstamping, which they view as an invasion of privacy. They feel background checks would require governments to keep databases of personal information on gun owners, although information collected during current NICS background checks must be destroyed by the next day. Microstamping is a technology used to identify individual weapons. A laser-imprinted engraving on the firing pin causes the gun's serial number to be stamped on each cartridge when the gun is fired. Investigators

A gun's serial number is microstamped in the center of each cartridge.

can then trace a gun from its spent cartridges without actually recovering the gun. Use of microstamping in this way requires a database of gun owners and their guns' serial numbers.

Most gun rights advocates focus on the individual right to own and use guns, not about the formation of militias, the older interpretation of the Second Amendment. However, there has been a recent upsurge in heavily armed right-wing extremist groups that carry out military-style training. These groups feel Second Amendment rights protect other freedoms by enabling armed uprisings to protect citizens from the "tyranny" of government authority. They feel "any form of gun regulation . . . is a sure sign of intent to crush other freedoms."[2] This philosophy is very similar to the current view of the NRA.

PRACTICAL REASONS AGAINST GUN CONTROL

In addition to defending their Second Amendment right to bear arms, many gun rights supporters also cite more practical reasons. For example, they say gun ownership, not gun control laws, deters crime. They cite several studies as evidence. During the 1900s, gun ownership doubled while the murder rate decreased.

Gun rights supporters believe criminals will obtain guns and break laws despite gun control laws. Criminals obtain guns illegally in several ways. The most common way is through straw purchases, where a companion buys the gun on the criminal's behalf. The second is through a licensed but corrupt gun dealer. The Federal Firearms Licensee (FFL) sells guns to gun traffickers, who in turn sell them to criminals. Other illegal guns are obtained from family and friends. Approximately 10 to 15 percent are stolen.[3] Finally, anti–gun control advocates note that, while Mexico has some of the world's strictest gun control laws, it also has one of the highest murder rates.

Gun rights supporters say these data suggest gun control is ineffective. Banning high-capacity magazines will not help because even low-capacity magazines can be changed rapidly. Closing the gun show loophole would be ineffective because most sellers at gun shows are commercial dealers who must obey already existing federal laws.

SOCIAL REASONS FOR GUN RIGHTS

While gun control supporters advocate gun control laws to prevent suicides and accidental deaths, gun rights supporters do not think these laws prevent either. They list a number of countries with low gun ownership rates but

IS THERE A GUN SHOW LOOPHOLE?

Gun control advocates cite "closing the gun show loophole" as one way to prevent criminals from obtaining illegal guns.[4] But the term is not precise. Gun rights advocates say it does not exist. Most people selling at gun shows are licensed dealers who must meet all federal requirements. Private sellers without a federal license do not have to meet these requirements. However, most do not sell at gun shows; they sell online or to friends or relatives. There are no restrictions on these sales in most states. One problem is that no law exists specifying how many guns a person must sell before needing a license.

high suicide rates. The United States has the highest gun ownership rate but only the twenty-sixth-highest suicide rate. Organizations that promote or teach gun use agree accidental gun deaths result from careless or improper use of firearms. They feel gun safety education, not gun control laws, will decrease accidental gun deaths.

Many gun rights supporters argue gun control laws are inherently racist. They point to a long history of racist gun laws in the United States and suggest this racism continues today. According to Charles Gallagher of LaSalle University, current gun control laws are typically founded on racial fears and are aimed at poor, inner-city black communities, whose residents are assumed to be more dangerous than whites.

MORE TO THE
STORY

GUN CONTROL
AND RACISM

Racism in gun control began before the United States was founded. The 1751 French Black Code stated Louisiana colonists should stop and, if necessary, beat "any black carrying any potential weapon, such as a cane." Colonists could "shoot to kill" blacks on horseback.[5] During the 1800s, to prevent slave revolts, slave states passed laws disarming blacks. Some laws specifically stated the Second Amendment did not apply to blacks because they were not citizens. The racist Ku Klux Klan began as a gun control organization after the American Civil War (1861–1865). Its goal was to reinforce white supremacy by seizing guns blacks had acquired during the war.

Another surge of racist gun control sentiment occurred in the 1960s. Besides high-profile political assassinations, the decade also had civil rights uprisings led by militant groups such as the Black Panthers. Many thought proposed gun control laws were designed to disarm black militants. Journalist Robert Sherrill said the purpose of the laws was "black control rather than gun control."[6] But this gun control movement also led to a backlash from white, rural conservatives who now form the backbone of today's gun rights movement.

CHAPTER SEVEN

THE VICTIMS OF
GUN VIOLENCE

During 2013, 33,636 people died of gunshot wounds in the United States. Of these, 21,175 were suicides. Another 502 were victims of mass shootings.[1] Most of the remainder were single homicides, with a few classified as either accidents or police shootings. According to research collected by the Harvard School of Public Health, many of these deaths could have been prevented by confiscating or restricting access to guns.

Shooting victims cannot be neatly classified. They are children and adults, men and women, and members of all races. Some fit into several groups.

Protestors outside the Capitol hold a sign listing some of the most recent gun violence incidents.

GUN DEATHS FROM SUICIDE

Suicides—the largest percentage of gun deaths—receive little attention. According to Jill Harkavy-Friedman of the American Foundation for Suicide Prevention, these deaths are often impulsive. They happen when mental health problems and easy access to guns combine. In 2010, three-fifths of all gun deaths were suicides.[2] This statistic is not unusual. Since 1920, suicides have outnumbered other causes of gun deaths nearly every year. For this reason, public health researchers want suicide to become a much larger part of the gun control debate.

> "IT IS REALLY, REALLY HARD TO SHOOT PEOPLE WHEN YOU DON'T HAVE A GUN."[3]
>
> —MICHAEL NUTTER, MAYOR OF PHILADELPHIA, ARGUING FOR GUN CONTROL

Cathy Barber, of the Harvard School of Public Health, says simply reducing access to guns would reduce suicide deaths. Studies confirm this. People living in households with guns are 17 times more likely to die of suicide than those in households without guns. In the South and the West, where approximately 50 percent of households have guns, people are almost four times more likely to kill themselves than those in states with 15 percent or less gun ownership.[4]

Some people argue that anyone who wants to commit suicide will find a way. Researchers counter that guns are more lethal than other methods; they do not allow backing out or changing one's mind. Between 85 and 90 percent of those who attempt suicide by gun succeed.[5] An article in the *New England Journal of Medicine* states that more than 90 percent of people who survive a first suicide attempt do not try again.[6]

US gun violence deaths and injuries, 2012

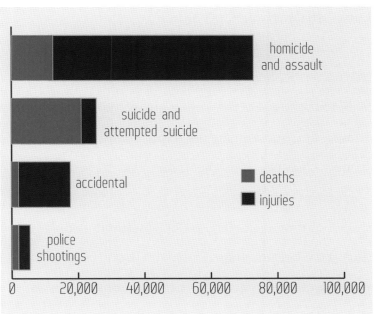

GUN DEATHS FROM DOMESTIC VIOLENCE

According to research by Everytown for Gun Safety, "Guns make it more likely that domestic abuse will turn into murder: When a gun is present in a domestic violence situation, it increases the risk of homicide for women by 500 percent." Women are 11 times more likely to be murdered by a gun in the United States than in any other developed country.[7] Boyfriends, husbands, or other family members commit more than half of these murders. An analysis of 2012 data by the Violence Policy Center showed 93 percent of female victims were killed by someone they knew, usually an intimate partner.[8]

Approximately 70 percent of mass shootings are also domestic shootings, occurring in people's homes. Sixty-four percent of the victims are women and children.[9] These mass shootings are not as publicized as shootings in schools, churches, and other public places.

A major difference between public and private mass shootings is predictability. In public settings, people usually die because they were in the wrong place at the wrong time. In domestic violence situations, deaths are often preceded by predictable factors. Experts say these warning signs make domestic abuse killings the most preventable types of homicides.

Federal and state laws include measures intended to keep guns out of the hands of domestic abusers and stalkers. When enforced properly, such laws save lives. In states requiring background checks for all gun sales, domestic partners shoot 38 percent fewer women.[10] But gaps and loopholes often prevent enforcement. Federal law prevents abusive husbands from buying or owning guns, but it says nothing about abusive boyfriends or convicted stalkers. If a man has not lived with, married,

Young urban black men are among the people hardest hit by gun violence.

or had a child with his partner, he is not considered an "intimate partner" and is not prevented from buying a gun, even though dating partners kill more women than spouses do. It is up to federal agents and prosecutors to enforce restrictions. Because of loopholes that allow gun purchases from unlicensed dealers online or at gun shows, domestic abusers and stalkers can easily evade the background checks required by federal law and most state laws. Forty-one states do not require convicted domestic abusers to give up guns they already own.[11]

GUN DEATHS AND RACE

During 2012, while mass shootings killed 90 people, nearly 6,000 black men also died from gun violence.[12] Between 1980 and 2013, 262,000 black men were shot to death on the streets of big cities.[13] A few are police interventions, particularly white police shooting black suspects. Many people are convinced police disproportionately target black men. Others say police kill more whites than blacks. Statistics are incomplete and vary widely on homicides and injuries due to police shootings. There are not

MORE TO THE
STORY

MICHAEL BROWN AND FERGUSON, MISSOURI

At approximately noon on August 9, 2014, 18-year-old Michael Brown and his friend Dorian Johnson left a liquor and convenience store in Ferguson, Missouri. Surveillance videos showed Brown stealing from the store. While walking down a nearby street, the two were challenged by white police officer Darren Wilson. After a confrontation, Wilson fired two shots from his police car and pursued Brown on foot and fired ten more times. Brown, who was black and unarmed, died on the street of gunshot wounds.

Witness accounts varied, but the shooting triggered racial protests that lasted for weeks. On November 24, the Saint Louis County prosecutor announced that a grand jury failed to find probable cause to charge Wilson with a crime. This set off even angrier protests, along with arson and looting. The Missouri National Guard was called in to restore order.

Brown's shooting led to a US Justice Department investigation, which uncovered many constitutional violations in the Ferguson criminal justice system. The report documented widespread police misconduct, including using racial insults, using stun guns without provocation, and stopping and handcuffing people without probable cause. After the report was released, the Ferguson police chief, Thomas Jackson, resigned.

precise numbers on the number of police homicides per year either.

Between 1999 and 2011, the CDC counted 2,151 whites and 1,130 blacks shot and killed by police. That is approximately twice as many whites. But whites outnumber blacks by 63 percent to 12 percent in the US population. A 2002 study showed police intervened in potentially violent situations three times as often when the person was black. When corrected for relative population sizes, felony rates for blacks are 1,178 per 100,000 for blacks and 330 per 100,000 for whites.[14]

After the Sandy Hook shooting, Michael McBride, a pastor from Berkeley, California, attended a White House conference on gun violence. McBride supported background checks and a ban on assault weapons. But he also wanted to make stopping urban violence, especially the killing of urban blacks, a priority. McBride promotes the program Ceasefire, in which police and community leaders identify young men at high risk of gun violence and offer them support and assistance. McBride was told the political will to address inner-city violence did not exist. He says most people assume "urban violence is a problem with black folk. It's not a problem for this country to solve." But in Boston, where Ceasefire began, youth homicide rates dropped 63 percent per month in the two years after its launch.[15]

Often, people seek simple solutions to gun violence. They want to control it by using the same method in all situations. But policy writer Christopher Ingraham cautions the situation is not this simple. Most gun deaths among black people are homicides; among white people, most are suicides. Black parents worry most about their children being shot; white parents worry about drug or alcohol abuse or depression. More than twice as many white as black families own guns. More whites than blacks think guns will protect them. Almost twice as many whites as blacks think protecting gun rights is more important than controlling gun ownership.[16] Because the amount and type of violence varies so much by race, no single policy approach will solve the issue.

"WHY DO WE ALLOW OUR CITIZENS TO KILL EACH OTHER AS IF IT'S THE COST OF DOING BUSINESS? WE HAVE BASICALLY GIVEN UP ON OUR AFRICAN AMERICAN BOYS."[17]

—MITCH LANDRIEU, MAYOR OF NEW ORLEANS

FROM THE HEADLINES

#BLACKLIVESMATTER

Trayvon Martin, Michael Brown, Eric Garner, Tamir Rice, Sandra Bland, Freddie Gray. All were African American. All were ordinary people. Now all are household names because they were shot or otherwise killed, mostly by white policemen. They are the faces of the #blacklivesmatter movement.

The movement began almost accidentally in July 2013. Alicia Garza was sad and angry about the not-guilty verdict for George Zimmerman, who had shot Martin. She posted an impassioned "love note to black people" on her Facebook page, ending with "Our lives matter."[18] Her friend Patrisse Cullors began reposting Garza's message, using the hashtag #blacklivesmatter. With the help of another friend, Opal Tometi, the three soon set up Tumblr and Twitter accounts and encouraged people to share their stories about why #blacklivesmatter. They staged local protests.

Subsequent shootings, including Michael Brown by a white policeman in Ferguson, Missouri, and nine black worshippers by a white supremacist in a Charleston church, energized the movement. #Blacklivesmatter emerged from gun violence against blacks, but it also highlights the damage done by racism and inequality in education, jobs, and voting rights. By 2016, there were at least 26 Black Lives Matter chapters across the United States. Garza's heartfelt Facebook post launched a new civil rights movement.

A man shows solidarity as he stands with the crowd at a Black Lives Matter rally.

CHAPTER EIGHT

GUN VIOLENCE
AROUND THE
WORLD

When considering the number of gun deaths in the United States every year and the number of innocent people killed, it is easy to assume the only solution is more gun control. And when a person is unable to buy a weapon because it is on a banned list, it is equally easy to blame gun laws for obstructing freedom. But is either viewpoint completely valid? One way to judge the need for, and effectiveness of, gun control is to compare the situation in the United States with that in other countries.

A collection of guns is on display after a police raid is completed in Toronto, Canada, in an effort to get semiautomatic weapons off the streets.

People in the United States own the most firearms per person of any country. The country has fewer than 5 percent of the world's people but between 35 and 50 percent of its guns.[1] It also has the highest rate of firearm homicides in all developed countries. Many gun rights advocates counter that more guns do not necessarily cause more homicides, and that gun crimes, including homicides, have declined since the early 1990s.

Similar to the United States, other countries have suffered horrifying massacres. Most have responded by quickly passing highly restrictive gun laws. Have these laws worked? How does crime in other countries compare with US crime?

CANADA

Canada's gun control laws are much stricter than US laws. All gun owners must have a license, which requires a background check. Owners must be at least 18 years old. Canada classifies firearms into three groups: "nonrestricted" (which includes most rifles and shotguns), "restricted" (handguns and some short rifles and shotguns), and "prohibited" (automatic weapons and

FIREARM COMPARISONS

These graphs compare two aspects of the gun culture in the United States and several other countries. The top graph shows number of guns per 100 citizens. The lower graph shows annual number of gun deaths per 100,000 citizens.[2]

Guns per 100 Citizens

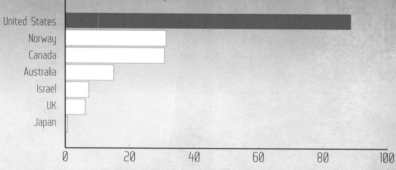

Guns Deaths per 100,000 Citizens

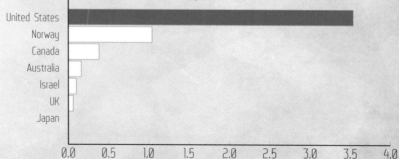

sawed-off rifles or shotguns). A person can buy a restricted weapon by obtaining a federal registration certificate.

Canada's gun laws are based on prior gun violence. In 1989, a shooter took a semiautomatic rifle into an engineering school, killed 14 women, and injured 14 more men and women.[3] He was angry about being denied admission to the school while women were admitted. This event led to the 1995 Firearms Act, which required all gun owners to be licensed and all long guns to be registered. It also banned more than half of all registered guns. The government abandoned the long-gun registry in 2012 due to high costs.

The Firearms Act decreased gun homicides. But when semiautomatic rifles were banned, street gangs turned to handguns. This led to stricter handgun registration, which further lowered crime rates. However, rates have not declined as much as hoped

GUN LAWS IN CANADA

All Canadian gun owners must be licensed, while all handguns and most semiautomatic weapons must be registered with the Royal Canadian Mounted Police. Handguns cannot be carried outside the home, either openly or concealed, without a specific license given to those using guns in their work. Before receiving a gun license, a person must be trained in gun safety and undergo an extensive background check. All guns must be kept locked and unloaded.

because many Canadian criminals can obtain handguns illegally from the United States.

AUSTRALIA

Australia also tightened gun control laws following a massacre. The worst mass shooting in the country's history occurred in April 1996 in Port Arthur, Tasmania. A young man wielding a semiautomatic rifle killed 35 people and wounded 23.[4] Only two weeks later, the government, with cooperation of the states, passed the National

Australian police sort and catalog firearms citizens turned in for refunds in 1997.

Agreement on Firearms. It prohibited nearly all automatic and semiautomatic assault rifles and strengthened both licensing and ownership rules. To obtain a license, people must demonstrate a "genuine need" for a gun and take a firearm safety course. Through a buyback program, in which citizens turned in their guns to the government and were paid the market value, the country removed 650,000 assault weapons, approximately one-sixth of the total, from circulation.[5] After another shooting in 2002, the country also tightened its handgun laws.

Total gun homicides have generally decreased in Australia since the 1996 law was passed. Handgun use in homicides was very high after 1996, until the laws were tightened. It has shown a steep decline since approximately 2005.

UNITED KINGDOM

The United Kingdom has had its share of deadly gun rampages. The 1987 Hungerford Massacre occurred 70 miles (110 km) west of London, England. A gunman with a semiautomatic weapon killed 16 people and then himself.[6] This led to the passage of the Firearms

(Amendment) Act, which added to the list of banned weapons and increased registration requirements for others. In 1996, in Dunblane, Scotland, a man armed with four legally purchased handguns killed 16 schoolchildren, an adult, and then himself.[7] This led to legislation banning almost all handguns. A gun buyback program removed more weapons from circulation. In general, the United Kingdom public supports the gun bans, but some sports shooters complain the laws prevent them from engaging in their hobby.

The effectiveness of the United Kingdom's gun control measures was not immediately obvious. As they were enacted, crime from street gangs using

IS THE UNITED NATIONS CONFISCATING OUR GUNS?

In April 2013, the UN General Assembly approved the Arms Trade Treaty (ATT), establishing standards for the import, export, and transfer of conventional arms. The United States voted in favor of the treaty; only three countries voted against it: Syria, North Korea, and Iran. The ATT is designed to stem the illegal trade of weapons across international borders and prevent arms from being used in human-rights violations, such as terrorism. But extreme right-wing organizations see the ATT as a plot by the United Nations and President Barack Obama to dismantle the Second Amendment and confiscate US guns. The fact-checking organization Snopes.com discredited both assertions. First, the ATT does not restrict the sale or trade of guns within individual countries, only across national borders. Second, the president has no power to ban weapons through international treaties; this would violate the Constitution. Third, treaties are only binding if approved by a two-thirds vote of Congress.

handguns and air weapons was also increasing. Handgun crime continued climbing for four years after the 1998 ban, but by 2013, handgun crime had declined by half and was showing a continuous decline. Criminologist Peter Squires thinks the decrease is due to a combination of improved legislation and better police response to gangs.

OTHER COUNTRIES

The European Union (EU) has adopted a framework to define legal gun ownership. The 1991 European Council Directive prohibits private citizens from possessing fully automatic weapons and strictly regulates possession of handguns and semiautomatic rifles and shotguns. People seeking to own a weapon must obtain a license, which requires undergoing a thorough background check and providing legitimate reasons for owning a gun. Each country has its own laws, which include differences in the ways licenses are obtained. In France, for example, a person must practice shooting for six months at an official shooting club and receive a favorable rating. This is followed by a criminal and mental health check. A passing score results in a gun license good for five years.

An instructor leads a group of Israeli men in a handgun training session.

Gun ownership is not a right in all countries, including France, Norway, and the United Kingdom. Penalties for having an illegal firearm vary. In France, a person might serve seven years in prison, but in Norway, only three months. No more than 30 percent of citizens in any European country own a gun, and they have correspondingly low death rates from gun violence.[8]

Other countries have very different gun cultures. In Israel, everyone enters military service and receives gun training at age 18. Guns are part of everyday life; they are treated with respect, and gun regulation is expected and accepted. After military service, Israelis must abide by civilian gun control laws. To obtain a gun license, a person must have Israeli citizenship or permanent residency, be at least age 21, and speak Hebrew. Firearms must be registered with the government, and the person must demonstrate a need for gun ownership.

Switzerland has the world's third-highest gun ownership rate. Young Swiss men are issued assault rifles or pistols for their military service and keep them at home. They keep the barrel and pistol in separate places, and ammunition is stored at a central arsenal. Unlike in the United States, Swiss guns are not meant for self-protection. Swiss soldiers are a citizen militia. Regardless, Swiss laws were tightened in 2006 after a high-profile shooting. Gun-related domestic homicides and suicides are higher in Switzerland than anywhere else in Europe except Finland.

In contrast, Japan has the world's lowest gun-homicide rate and the most restrictive gun policies. Most guns are illegal, and people must receive formal instruction to use any gun. They must pass written, mental, and drug tests and a strict background check. They must tell authorities how they store the gun and ammunition, and they must submit the gun for an annual inspection.

It appears that, in most other countries, stricter gun control policies and limited access to guns translate to very low rates of gun violence. In Switzerland and Israel, although many citizens have guns, strict gun control laws, respect for weapons, and good training combine to keep gun violence low. Squires points out that gun control laws in any country are only one aspect of crime prevention. He acknowledges that criminals break gun laws, but this does not invalidate using these laws in crime prevention. The main objective, he says, is to find "the most effective series of gun violence prevention measures" while maintaining other important values of society.[9] Squires emphasizes that a highly cohesive, tolerant, trusting, and responsible society has little to fear from gun ownership. However, the more divisive a society is, the more hazardous firearms become. In the early 2000s, most people agree US culture is highly divided on many issues, including gun control.

"SOCIETIES UNDERGOING RAPID SOCIAL CHANGES, OR RIVEN WITH CONFLICTS AND DIVISIONS ARE LIKELY TO BECOME INCREASINGLY DANGEROUS WHEN FIREARMS ARE ADDED TO THE MIX. UNFORTUNATELY THESE SOCIETIES ARE OFTEN THE VERY PLACES WHERE PRIVATE CITIZENS SEEK FIREARMS FOR 'SELF-DEFENCE' PURPOSES."[10]

—PETER SQUIRES,
BRITISH CRIMINOLOGIST

CHAPTER NINE

THE FUTURE OF
GUN CONTROL

The future of gun control involves complex questions. How will public attitudes change or stay the same? Will the NRA retain its power? Will opposing sides remain angry, divided, and deadlocked, or will they rediscover the art of compromise? Will the courts take on the Second Amendment, and if so, what will they decide? Finally, what new technologies might affect gun control?

THE NRA AND THE FUTURE OF GUN CONTROL

In April 2013, five months after the Sandy Hook shooting, the US Senate voted on whether to increase background checks on gun buyers. The vote failed

With hundreds of shootings occurring in the United States weekly, many Americans want the NRA to have less control over legislation.

STOP

the

NRA

CREDO
actio

by five votes, leading many people to conclude the NRA was controlling votes in the legislature. Polls showed 90 percent of Americans wanted the bill to pass.[1] Some senators who voted "no" saw their approval ratings go down. When they went home, they faced irate voters.

There is no question the NRA has tremendous power. It bankrolls elections and shapes public opinion. It has taken partial credit for deciding presidential elections, including George W. Bush's win in 2000. More recently, the NRA has sought to influence the choice of judicial nominees, a traditionally nonpartisan process. After the election of President Barack Obama, Senate Republicans

The NRA's power has helped keep gun stores open and keep sales at a steady pace.

worked closely with the NRA to help discredit his Supreme Court nominees based on their gun control records. This was difficult with Elena Kagan and Sonia Sotomayor, since neither had judged gun control cases. Regardless, both were confirmed with almost no Republican backing. But the Senate, based on the NRA's opposition, did block the appointment of one of Obama's lower-court nominees. Caitlin Halligan, a lawyer from New York, had worked on one case representing the state against gun manufacturers and had written a brief for the state's attorney general holding gun manufacturers liable for some of New York's gun violence. According to Jeff Toobin in the *New Yorker*, "The NRA punished Halligan for doing her job in New York."[2]

Some people think the NRA is stronger than ever. Dave Saunders, a Democratic strategist and gun owner, says, "Every time a Democrat starts talking about guns, they lose numbers because it is the Second Amendment."[3] But *New Republic* writer Alec MacGillis disagrees. He says, "For some time now, the NRA's power has been more a matter of entrenched wisdom than actual fact." US gun ownership has declined from half of households in the 1970s to only one-third in 2013. The NRA's ratings of elected officials do not always determine whether they are elected. Recently, some anti-NRA senators and governors were elected, and in 2012, 13 of 16 candidates supported by the NRA lost.[4] Gun control expert Winkler thinks public support for the NRA will decline.

THE JUDICIAL APPROACH

The public and the NRA can pressure legislators to enact or not enact gun control measures. In addition, state courts and the Supreme Court will continue to interpret the Second Amendment. Legal expert Michael J. Habib states that the Supreme Court's consideration of the Second Amendment is just beginning, and many questions remain unanswered. He expects the recent decisions in *Heller* and *McDonald*, which extended Second Amendment rights to individuals, will result in many future decisions at both the state and federal levels. Habib hopes these decisions will strike down many gun control laws he finds restrictive, for example, laws that restrict handgun purchases to one per month.

Sarah Brady, the wife of James Brady, speaks on the importance of the Brady Handgun Violence Prevention Act.

So far, the Supreme Court has chosen not to hear a number of Second Amendment cases, which means the lower court rulings on these cases remain accepted law. According to expert Joseph Blocher, this frustrates gun rights advocates, many of whom think lower courts are failing to enforce Second Amendment rights. Brian Doherty, of the Libertarian Reason Foundation, lists several such cases the Supreme Court chose not to hear between the 2008 *Heller* case and 2012. In 2015, the Supreme Court chose not to hear a case that might have broadened the interpretation of the Second Amendment. In the 2015 case, the NRA argued the Second Amendment was violated by a Chicago suburb's ban on semiautomatic weapons and high-capacity magazines. The court's refusal to hear the case affirmed the lower court's decision not to expand Second Amendment protections. Thus, the NRA lost when the Supreme Court signaled that Second Amendment freedoms could be extended only so far.

ARE ATTITUDES CHANGING?

Although Congress has failed to act, state governments are beginning to take action to strengthen gun control. In the year following the Sandy Hook shooting, eight states passed gun reform laws. In 2014, Washington overwhelmingly approved universal background checks for all gun purchases. In 2015, several states voted to restrict domestic abusers' access to firearms. A group of 2,000 doctors is urging Congress to repeal the Dickey Amendment, passed in 1996 under pressure from the NRA.[5] This amendment prevents the CDC from researching gun violence, limiting the data available. Between 2012 and 2014, gun control groups such as Americans for Responsible Solutions raised more money than gun rights groups such as the NRA. These factors suggest support for gun control is increasing in the United States, and the strength of the NRA is waning.

For decades, the NRA has offered relentless, single-minded opposition to gun control. But until the Sandy Hook shooting, it had little organized opposition. That event mobilized gun control advocates in a way thousands of single gun homicides, and even previous mass shootings, never did. People are becoming less willing to accept gun violence. Sandy Hook activists have combined with the gun control movement spearheaded by Michael Bloomberg, former mayor of New York City. Bloomberg is not discouraged by setbacks such as the failure of the national background check vote. He takes a longer view and knows this work will take time.

AMERICANS FOR RESPONSIBLE SOLUTIONS

In January 2011, US Representative Gabrielle Giffords (D-AZ) was shot in the head while holding a meeting with constituents in Tucson, Arizona. Six people were killed and 13, including Gifford, were injured in the mass shooting. Giffords underwent a long recovery and continued rehabilitation. She resigned from Congress and, with her husband, retired astronaut Mark Kelly, founded Americans for Responsible Solutions. They started this super political action committee (super-PAC) to counter the political activity of the NRA. The organization raised $6.5 million in its first six months, much of it from small and medium-sized donors.[6] In 2016, the group merged with the San Francisco legal group Law Center to Prevent Gun Violence. "By coming together we can do more to take on the gun lobby, deliver even more victories for common sense, and save lives," said Giffords and Kelly in a joint statement.[7]

NEXT GENERATION: THE SMART GUN?

The future of gun control depends on more than political, legal, and citizen action. It also involves changes in technology. A major new technology, the smart gun, can be fired only by its owner. It contains a computer chip keyed to a watch worn by the owner, who must enter a PIN code to fire it. If the gun is stolen, the thief cannot use it without knowing the PIN. The gun also deactivates after a specified time. Nearly 60 percent of US handgun buyers say they are willing to buy a smart gun.[8]

Other technologies include new methods of locking up guns that are smaller and smarter than the typical gun safe. Armatrix, a German smart gun manufacturer, makes locks that insert into gun barrels and prevent firing. As with smart guns, the gun is fired by inputting a PIN code. The Las Vegas, Nevada, company GunVault makes the ARVault, which locks over only the working parts of the semiautomatic AR-15. The lock is activated by fingerprints and opens when the owner places a hand in the hand-shaped space on the vault. A similar device, the IdentiLock, covers only the trigger and trigger guard of the gun. To release the lock, the owner places a fingertip over a sensor just above the trigger.

The gun control story is ongoing, and any summary of future trends is necessarily incomplete. More than many issues, gun control is subject to changing events, from shootings to elections to the actions of citizens. People concerned about gun control issues should stay informed, learn to distinguish between facts and propaganda on both sides, and actively support the policies they find most reasonable.

STOPPING THE SMART GUN

In the 1990s, two gun manufacturers, Colt and Smith & Wesson, planned to develop smart guns. But the NRA criticized this idea. It said such technologies would allow gun control advocates to target gun manufacturers. This worried consumers, who staged a boycott of Smith & Wesson. In 2005, the NRA pressured Congress to pass the Protection of Lawful Commerce in Arms Act. This limited the legal liability of gun manufacturers for failing to implement safer ways to design or distribute guns. It also gave manufacturers less reason to develop smart guns. In 2016, the NRA did not oppose smart guns but worried the technology would make guns more expensive and allow the guns to be disabled remotely.

ESSENTIAL
FACTS

MAJOR EVENTS

- The Bill of Rights passes on September 25, 1789, and the states ratify it on December 15, 1791. The Second Amendment is the right to bear arms.

- The National Firearms Act passes in 1934, targeting fully automatic weapons and sawed-off shotguns.

- The Gun Control Act passes in 1968, increasing licensing requirements for gun sellers and prohibiting mail-order sales of rifles and shotguns.

- The Brady Handgun Violence Prevention Act is signed in 1993, and the Violent Crime Control and the Assault Weapons Ban pass in 1994.

KEY PLAYERS

- Colonel William C. Church and General George Wingate found the National Rifle Association (NRA) in 1871.

- Neal Knox and Harlon Carter engineer the Revolt at Cincinnati in 1997, which turns the NRA into a political lobbying organization to stop all efforts at gun control.

- Gabrielle Giffords and Mark Kelly start Americans for Responsible Solutions, a super-PAC supporting political candidates favoring gun control.

IMPACT ON SOCIETY

The Second Amendment is interpreted primarily in two different ways, leading to a highly polarized society. Gun rights advocates believe individuals have the right to own an unlimited number of guns of any kind, and gun control advocates believe gun ownership and use should be carefully regulated. In recent decades, the polarization has become extreme. Due at least in part to easy access to weapons, gun violence is very high. This violence is most pronounced in poor, urban neighborhoods, where it disproportionately affects blacks and other minorities, as well as women and children. But the greatest media coverage is given to mass shootings, which have occurred with greater frequency in recent years.

QUOTE

"Societies undergoing rapid social changes, or riven with conflicts and divisions are likely to become increasingly dangerous when firearms are added to the mix. Unfortunately these societies are often the very places where private citizens seek firearms for 'self-defence' purposes."

—Peter Squires, British criminologist

GLOSSARY

AIR WEAPON
An air rifle, air gun, or air pistol, which does not contain any explosive substance.

AUTOMATIC WEAPON
A firearm, such as a machine gun, that fires continuously with a single pull of the trigger.

LIBERTARIAN
A person who believes in the doctrine of free will and upholds liberty in thought and action.

LOBBYING ORGANIZATION
An organization that tries to convince government officials to vote in a certain way.

MILITIA
A military force made up of nonprofessional fighters.

PUBLIC POLICY
A government policy that affects the whole population of a country.

RIGHT WING
A conservative, traditional, or reactionary political group that, among other beliefs, considers social equity to be the natural and inevitable result of economic competition.

SEMIAUTOMATIC WEAPON
A weapon that fires a single shot with every pull of the trigger, but automatically reloads from a magazine between shots.

STANDING ARMY
A permanent, professional army composed of full-time soldiers, which is not disbanded during peacetime.

STRAW PURCHASE
An illegal gun purchase made by a family member, friend, or acquaintance on behalf of a criminal, juvenile, or other person not legally eligible to buy a firearm.

ADDITIONAL
RESOURCES

SELECTED BIBLIOGRAPHY

Cook, Philip J., and Kristin A. Goss. *The Gun Debate: What Everyone Needs to Know*. Oxford: Oxford UP, 2014. Print.

Masters, Jonathan. "Gun Control around the World: A Primer." *Atlantic*. Atlantic Monthly Group, 12 Jan. 2016. Web. 8 July 2016.

"Should More Gun Control Laws Be Enacted?" *ProCon.org*. ProCon.org, 2016. Web. 8 July 2016.

Winkler, Adam. *Gunfight: The Battle over the Right to Bear Arms in America*. New York: Norton, 2013. Print.

FURTHER READINGS

Merino, Noël, ed. *Gun Control*. Farmington Hills, MI: Greenhaven, 2015. Print.

Nakaya, Andrea C. *Mass Shootings*. San Diego: ReferencePoint, 2016. Print.

WEBSITES

To learn more about Special Reports, visit **booklinks.abdopublishing.com**. These links are routinely monitored and updated to provide the most current information available.

FOR MORE INFORMATION

For more information on this subject, contact or visit the following organizations:

The Coalition to Stop Gun Violence
805 15th Street Northwest
Washington, DC 20005
202-408-0061
http://csgv.org
This gun control organization is a coalition of 47 agencies. They undertake educational, policy-based, and political action.

Second Amendment Foundation
12500 Northeast 10th Place
Bellevue, WA 98005
425-454-7012
http://www.saf.org
This gun rights organization uses educational and legal action campaigns to inform people about the Second Amendment and promote gun rights issues.

SOURCE
NOTES

CHAPTER 1. MASSACRE AT SANDY HOOK

1. Tracy Connor. "'Call for Everything': Police Scanner Recording Reveals Early Moments of Newtown Tragedy." *NBC News*. NBC News, 19 Dec. 2012. Web. 8 July 2016.

2. Susan Candiotti and Sarah Aarthun. "Police: 20 Children Among 26 Victims of Connecticut School Shooting." *CNN*. Cable News Network, 15 Dec. 2012. Web. 8 July 2016.

3. "Sandy Hook Promise." Sandy Hook Promise, 2015. Web. 8 July 2016.

4. "School Safety Legislation Since Newtown." *Education Week*. Editorial Projects, 24 Apr. 2013. Web. 8 July 2016.

5. "UC Davis Report Exposes Loopholes in Gun-control Laws." UC Davis Health System. UC Regents, 2016. Web. 8 July 2016.

6. Frank Newport. "Americans Wanted Gun Background Checks to Pass Senate." *Gallup*. Gallup, 29 Apr. 2013. Web. 8 July 2016.

7. Ben Smart. "School Shootings, Mass Killings are 'Contagious,' Study Finds." *CNN*. Cable News Network, 3 Nov. 2015. Web. 8 July 2016.

8. German Lopez. "The UCLA Shooting Exposes How We Often Ignore the Most Common Forms of Gun Violence." *Vox*. Vox Media, 1 June 2016. Web. 8 July 2016.

9. Jennifer Mascia. "15 Statistics That Tell the Story of Gun Violence This Year." *Trace*. Trace, 23 Dec. 2015. Web. 8 July 2016.

10. "Key Gun Violence Statistics." *Brady Campaign to Prevent Gun Violence*. Brady Campaign to Prevent Gun Violence, 2016. Web. 8 July 2016.

11. David Kyle Johnson. "Guns Don't Kill People, People Do?" *Psychology Today*. Sussex, 12 Feb. 2013. Web. 8 July 2016.

12. Ibid.

CHAPTER 2. THE SECOND AMENDMENT

1. Nelson Lund and Adam Winkler. "The Second Amendment." *Constitution Center*. National Constitution Center, n.d. Web. 8 July 2016.

2. Saul Cornell and Nathan DeDino. "A Well-Regulated Right: The Early American Origins of Gun Control." *Fordham Law Review*. Fordham Law Archive, 2004. Web. 8 July 2016.

3. Henry Blodget. "Look, Can We Please At Least Agree On One Thing About the 'Right To Bear Arms'?" *Business Insider*. Business Insider, 23 July 2012. Web. 8 July 2016.

4. "U.S. and World Population Clock." *United States Census Bureau*. US Department of Commerce, 11 July 2016. Web. 8 July 2016.

5. Henry Blodget. "Look, Can We Please At Least Agree On One Thing About the 'Right To Bear Arms'?" *Business Insider*. Business Insider, 23 July 2012. Web. 8 July 2016.

6. Philip J. Cook and Kristin A. Goss. *The Gun Debate*. Oxford: Oxford UP, 2014. Print. 5.

7. Nelson Lund. "Not a Second-Class Right: The Second Amendment Today." *Constitution Center*. National Constitution Center, n.d. Web. 8 July 2016.

8. Ibid.

9. Adam Winkler. "The Reasonable Right to Bear Arms." *Constitution Center*. National Constitution Center, n.d. Web. 8 July 2016.

10. John Paul Stevens. "The Five Extra Words That Can Fix the Second Amendment." *Washington Post*. Washington Post, 11 Apr. 2014. Web. 8 July 2016.

11. Adam Winkler. "The Reasonable Right to Bear Arms." *Constitution Center*. National Constitution Center, n.d. Web. 8 July 2016.

12. Ibid.

13. Ibid.

14. "District of Columbia et al. v. Heller." *Legal Information Institute*. Cornell University Law School, 26 June 2008. Web. 8 July 2016.

15. Ibid.

CHAPTER 3. A SHORT HISTORY OF GUN CONTROL

1. Philip J. Cook and Kristin A. Goss. *The Gun Debate*. Oxford: Oxford UP, 2014. Print. 164.

2. Robert J Spitzer. "Five Myths About Gun Control." *Washington Post*. Washington Post, 21 Dec. 2012. Web. 8 July 2016.

3. Adam Winkler. *Gunfight: The Battle over the Right to Bear Arms in America*. New York: Norton, 2013. Print. 95–96.

4. Aaron Smith. "This is How Easy It is To Buy Guns in America." *CNN Money*. Cable News Network, 19 June 2015. Web. 8 July 2016.

5. Joseph A. Califano Jr. "Gun Control Lessons From Lyndon Johnson." *Washington Post*. Washington Post, 16 Dec. 2012. Web. 8 July 2016.

6. Tim Jones. "JFK Assassination Sowed Seeds of Failure for Gun Control Efforts." *Chicago Tribune*. Chicago Tribune, 26 Dec. 2015. Web. 8 July 2016.

7. Justine McDaniel et al. "Decades Old Gun Control Debate Reshaped by New Advocacy Groups." *Center for Public Integrity*. Center for Public Integrity, 21 Aug. 2014. Web. 8 July 2016.

CHAPTER 4. THE RISE OF THE NRA

1. Lily Rothman. "The Original Reason the NRA Was Founded." *Time*. Time, 17 Nov. 2015. Web. 8 July 2016.

2. Steven Rosenfeld. "The Surprising Unknown History of the NRA." *AlterNet*. AlterNet, 13 Jan. 2013. Web. 8 July 2016.

3. Ibid.

4. Ibid.

5. "For Most of Its History, the NRA Actually Backed Sensible Gun Regulation." *BoldProgressives.org*. PCCC, 17 Jan. 2013. Web. 8 July 2016.

6. Joel Achenbach et al. "How NRA's True Believers Converted a Marksmanship Group into a Mighty Gun Lobby." *Washington Post*. Washington Post, 12 Jan. 2013. Web. 8 July 2016.

7. Steven Rosenfeld. "The Surprising Unknown History of the NRA." *AlterNet*. AlterNet, 13 Jan. 2013. Web. 8 July 2016.

8. Michael Powell. "The NRA's Call to Arms." *Washington Post*. Washington Post, 6 Aug. 2000. Web. 8 July 2016.

9. Adam Winkler. "The NRA Will Fall. It's Inevitable." *Washington Post*. Washington Post, 19 Oct. 2015. 8 July 2016.

10. Joel Achenbach et al. "How NRA's True Believers Converted a Marksmanship Group into a Mighty Gun Lobby." *Washington Post*. Washington Post, 12 Jan. 2013. Web. 8 July 2016.

11. Craig Johnson and Sonia Kose. "Trayvon Martin's Death: How the Story Unfolded." HLN. Cable News Network, 5 Feb. 2016. Web. 8 July 2016.

CHAPTER 5. REASONS FOR GUN CONTROL

1. Philip J. Cook and Kristin A. Goss. *The Gun Debate*. Oxford: Oxford UP, 2014. Print. 5.

2. "Should More Gun Control Laws Be Enacted?" *ProCon.org*. ProCon.org, 2016. Retrieved Web. 8 July 2016.

3. Ibid.

4. Jacob Schuman. "The Equality Argument for Gun Control." *Huffington Post*. TheHuffingtonPost.com, 4 Nov. 2015. Web. 8 July 2016.

SOURCE NOTES
CONTINUED

5. "Should More Gun Control Laws Be Enacted?" *ProCon.org*. ProCon.org, 2016. Retrieved Web. 8 July 2016.

6. Philip J. Cook and Kristin A. Goss. *The Gun Debate*. Oxford: Oxford UP, 2014. Print. 18.

7. Robert Parry. "The Second Amendment's Fake History." *Consortiumnews.com*. Consortium News, 7 Oct. 2015. Web. 8 July 2016.

8. "Should More Gun Control Laws Be Enacted?" *ProCon.org*. ProCon.org, 2016. Retrieved Web. 8 July 2016.

9. Robert Parry. "The Second Amendment's Fake History." *Consortiumnews.com*. Consortium News, 7 Oct. 2015. Web. 8 July 2016.

10. Christine Jamieson. "Gun Violence Research." *American Psychological Association*. American Psychological Association, Feb. 2013. Web. 8 July 2016.

11. Ralph Ellis et al. "Orlando Shooting: What Motivated a Killer?" CNN. Cable News Network, 14 June 2016. Web. 8 July 2016.

12. Ibid.

CHAPTER 6. REASONS AGAINST GUN CONTROL

1. Philip J. Cook and Kristin A. Goss. *The Gun Debate*. Oxford: Oxford UP, 2014. Print. 4–5.

2. Dennis A. Henigan. "Right-Wing Militias and the NRA: Second Amendment Soulmates." *Huffington Post*. TheHuffingtonPost.com, 25 May 2011. Web. 8 July 2016.

3. Dan Noyes. "How Criminals Get Guns." *Frontline*. WGBH, 2014. Web. 8 July 2016.

4. Amy Sherman. "PolitiFact Sheet: 3 Things to Know About the 'Gun Show Loophole.'" *PolitiFact*. Tampa Bay Times, 7 Jan. 2016. Web. 8 July 2016.

5. Clayton E. Cramer. "The Racist Roots of Gun Control." *Shade's Landing*. Clayton E. Cramer, 1993. Web. 8 July 2016.

6. "The Truth About Gun Control, Racism and Genocide." *American Civil Rights Union*. American Civil Rights Union, 2015. Web. 8 July 2016.

CHAPTER 7. THE VICTIMS OF GUN VIOLENCE

1. German Lopez. "The UCLA Shooting Exposes How We Often Ignore the Most Common Forms of Gun Violence." *Vox*. Vox Media, 1 June 2016. Web. 8 July 2016.

2. Leon Neyfakh. "The Gun Toll We're Ignoring: Suicide." *Boston Globe*. Boston Globe Media Partner, 20 Jan. 2013. Web. 8 July 2016.

3. Jeffrey Goldberg. "A Matter of Black Lives." *Atlantic*. Atlantic Monthly Group, Sept. 2015. Web. 8 July 2016.

4. Leon Neyfakh. "The Gun Toll We're Ignoring: Suicide." *Boston Globe*. Boston Globe Media Partner, 20 Jan. 2013. Web. 8 July 2016.

5. Ibid.

6. Matthew Miller et al. "Guns and Suicide in the United States." *New England Journal of Medicine*. Massachusetts Medical Society, 4 Sept. 2008. Web. 8 July 2016.

7. "Guns and Violence Against Women." *Everytown for Gun Safety Support Fund.* Everytown for Gun Safety Support Fund, 16 June 2014. Web. 8 July 2016.

8. Josh Sugarmann. "For Women, Gun Violence Often Linked to Domestic Violence." *Huffington Post.* TheHuffingtonPost.com, 1 Dec. 2014. Web. 8 July 2016.

9. Ibid.

10. "Guns and Violence Against Women." *Everytown for Gun Safety Support Fund.* Everytown for Gun Safety Support Fund, 16 June 2014. Web. 8 July 2016.

11. Ibid.

12. Lois Beckett. "How the Gun Control Debate Ignores Black Lives." *ProPublica.* ProPublica, 24 Nov. 2015. Web. 8 July 2016.

13. Jeffrey Goldberg. "A Matter of Black Lives." *Atlantic.* Atlantic Monthly Group, Sept. 2015. Web. 8 July 2016.

14. John Greenberg. "Talk Show Host: Police Kill More Whites Than Blacks." *PunditFact.* Tampa Bay Times, 21 Aug. 2014. Web. 8 July 2016.

15. Lois Beckett. "How the Gun Control Debate Ignores Black Lives." *ProPublica.* ProPublica, 24 Nov. 2015. Web. 8 July 2016.

16. Jeffrey Goldberg. "A Matter of Black Lives." *Atlantic.* Atlantic Monthly Group, Sept. 2015. Web. 8 July 2016.

17. Christopher Ingraham. "The Shocking Difference in How Blacks and Whites Are Killed By Guns." *Washington Post.* Washington Post, 18 Dec. 2015. Web. 8 July 2016.

18. Elizabeth Day. "#BlackLivesMatter: The Birth of a New Civil Rights Movement." *Guardian.* Guardian News, 19 July 2015. Web. 8 July 2016.

CHAPTER 8. GUN VIOLENCE AROUND THE WORLD

1. Jonathan Masters. "Gun Control around the World: A Primer." *Atlantic.* Atlantic Monthly Group, 12 Jan. 2016. Web. 8 July 2016.

2. Ibid.

3. Julie Bindel. "The Montreal Massacre: Canada's Feminists Remember." *Guardian.* Guardian News, 3 Dec. 2012. Web. 8 July 2016.

4. Jonathan Masters. "Gun Control around the World: A Primer." *Atlantic.* Atlantic Monthly Group, 12 Jan. 2016. Web. 8 July 2016.

5. Ibid.

6. Ibid.

7. Ibid.

8. Guttman, Robert. "Gun Control (Europe) vs. Out of Control (United States)." *TransAtlantic.* Aug. 6, 2012. Retrieved May 20, 2016.

9. Peter Squires. "Hard Evidence: Does Gun Control Work?" *Conversation.* Conversation US, 19 Sept. 2013. Web. 8 July 2016.

10. Ibid.

CHAPTER 9. THE FUTURE OF GUN CONTROL

1. Alec MacGillis. "This Is How the NRA Ends." *New Republic.* New Republic, 27 May 2013. Web. 8 July 2016.

2. Mike Spies. "The NRA's New Playbook for Making Gun-Grabbers Out of Democratic Nominees." *Trace.* Trace, 17 Mar. 2016. Web. 8 July 2016.

3. Seth McLaughlin. "Obama-Bloomberg Gun Control Agenda Worries Democrats Heading into 2016." *Washington Times.* Washington Times, 9 Apr. 2015. Web. 8 July 2016.

4. Alec MacGillis. "This Is How the NRA Ends." *New Republic.* New Republic, 27 May 2013. Web. 8 July 2016.

5. Delphine D'Amora. "6 Signs the NRA Is Losing Its Stranglehold on Gun Policy." *Mother Jones.* Mother Jones, 10 Dec. 2015. Web. 8 July 2016.

6. Paul Blumenthal. "Gabrielle Giffords Gun Control Super PAC Raises $6.5 Million." *Huffington Post.* TheHuffingtonPost.com, 31 July 2013. Web. 8 July 2016.

7. Bill Theobald. "Gabrielle Giffords' Gun Control Group Merges with Calif. Group." *USA Today.* USA Today, 16 Mar. 2016. Web. 8 July 2016.

8. Josh Harkinson. "Welcome to the Future of Gun Control." *Mother Jones.* Mother Jones, Mar./Apr. 2016. Web. 8 July 2016.

9. Alec MacGillis. "This Is How the NRA Ends." *New Republic.* New Republic, 27 May 2013. Web. 8 July 2016.

INDEX

ABOUT THE
AUTHOR

Carol Hand has a PhD in zoology. She has taught college biology, written assessments and curricula for middle and high school, and authored more than 30 young adult books on science and social studies. She has followed the gun debate and hopes future policy will be based on reason and evidence.